"Mormon's Map" shows the mo
Nephite and Lamanite geographicaı ıeaɩuıes ʋaɔeu ʋıı aıı ɩııɕ
information in the record of Mormon and his son Moroni₂.
(Capitalization of names follows the practice of the published
text of the Book of Mormon.)

LEGEND
  1. waters of Ripliancum
  2. limit of Nephite retreat
  3. Shiz's death; plates left
  4. hill Shim
  5. narrow pass or passage
  6. Hagoth's shipbuilding site
  7. Moroni₁'s camp
  8. Nephites' refuge between the land Bountiful and the land
     of Zarahemla (see 3 Nephi 3:23, 25)
  9. hill Onidah
 10. hill Amnihu
 11. hill Riplah
 12. valley of Alma
 13. dispersal point of the sons of Mosiah₂
 14. waters of Mormon
 15. hill north of Shilom
 16. mount Antipas
 17. place Onidah
 18. wilderness on the west of the land Zarahemla
 19. wilderness on the west in the land of Nephi
 20. Lamanite king's land
 21. land of first inheritance
 22. wilderness (see Alma 43:22)
 23. mountain pass
 24. Hagoth's likely destination
 25. wilderness of Hermounts
 26. "line" between Desolation and Bountiful
 27. defense "line"

  • settlement
  ☐ land, no city mentioned
)(mountain pass
  ⋎ⲛⲱ swamp

River tributaries illustrative only.
Darker color indicates higher elevation.

MORMON'S MAP

MORMON'S MAP

John L. Sorenson

The Foundation for Ancient Research and Mormon Studies (FARMS)
at Brigham Young University
Provo, Utah

Cover design by Bjorn W. Pendleton
Maps by Robert W. Fullmer and Bjorn W. Pendleton

John L. Sorenson earned a Ph.D. in anthropology from the University of
California at Los Angeles. He is emeritus professor of anthropology at Brigham
Young University.

The Foundation for Ancient Research and Mormon Studies (FARMS)
at Brigham Young University
P.O. Box 7113
University Station
Provo, Utah 84602

Printed in the United States of America
07 06 05 04 03   6 5 4 3 2

Library of Congress Cataloging-in-Publication Data

Sorenson, John L.
    Mormon's Map / John L. Sorenson
        p.   cm.
    Includes bibliographical references and index.
    ISBN 0-934893-48-9 (pbk. : alk. paper)
        1. Book of Mormon—Geography. I. Title.

    BX8627 .S646 2000
    289.3'22—dc21

                                                        99-859013

Contents

*M*aps

$\mathcal{A}$cknowledgments

My particular thanks go to Robert W. Fullmer, my assistant, for preparing the maps and more; Bryan DeWitt and Stewart Brewer for preparing working papers of value to this project; Mary Mahan, manuscript editor for FARMS, for significant rephrasings and helpful comments; Bjorn Pendleton for design; Mel Thorne for overall supervision of editing and frequent encouragement; and Richard Hartley for seeing to the issuance of a separate master map.

I also appreciate the FARMS officers and board for supporting publication of this book.

Finally I express gratitude to my wife, Helen Lance Christianson, for her comments on early drafts of this manuscript as well as her consistent belief in the importance of my work.

chapter 1

Does Geography in the Book of Mormon Matter?

The Book of Mormon has been called "the keystone of our religion,"[1] and for Latter-day Saints it thus deserves no less than the deepest understanding of it we can obtain. Brigham Young has suggested the level of understanding we should aspire to: "Do you read the scriptures . . . as though you were writing them . . . ? Do you read them as though you stood in the place of the men who wrote them?"[2] What advantages do we have if we follow Brigham Young's advice?

The Book of Mormon was given to us through a very real artifact—a set of gold plates that were seen and "hefted" by a dozen or more witnesses. In contrast, the Bible reached us via generations of unknown hands, and we must wonder which portions of it were shaped by the human instruments through whom it was transmitted. We place high value on the Nephite scripture because of its tangible origin. Yet the sense of reality and concreteness we feel is weakened in part by the fact that Latter-day Saints as a body of believers have not been prepared to say where particular Nephite cities and mountains and streams are located. We can visit Bethlehem's hills and feel that we are standing where the Jewish shepherds did when the angels spoke to them, but on tours to "Book of Mormon lands" we are unable to say with confidence, "Here Alma and Amulek were imprisoned," or "Through this valley tramped Helaman's two thousand warriors." Would not our sense of the reality of the Nephites and their sacred book be enhanced if we could share with Mormon his map of the scenes where the events he wrote about took place? The sense of reality with which we envision the events, scenes, and characters in the Book of Mormon can be intensified to the degree that we pin down the geographical setting.

The Nephite scripture promises its readers sacred knowledge that can transform their personal lives. To receive that blessing, we as readers must connect ourselves as forcefully as possible to what the ancient writers of the scripture tell us. Only by relating intimately to them and their words can we receive the power they sought to convey to us. The scriptures are meant to cause us to "lift up [our] hearts and rejoice" (2 Nephi 11:8), and we cannot fully do that without penetrating as thoroughly as possible what was in the hearts and minds of the scripture makers at the time they wrote. We cannot be impacted to the maximum by their message unless we can empathize with their pains, puzzle over their problems, and join in their joys. The ancient prophets have something of great value to confer on people across all generations and cultures because they, more clearly than most humans, have identified and wrestled with the frustrations, despairs, and pains that afflict us all: What is this seemingly senseless life really about? Is death the end? How can I achieve the greatest happiness? Why am I hated, in pain, starved, depressed? These ancient prophets stir our interest and awaken our hopes because, while they were each a fallible everyman, like us plagued with questions, they testify boldly that they found answers.

But we cannot fully share the light that transformed their lives until we grasp in specific terms, not just in vaguely theoretical ones, what the questions meant to them. We cannot fully "liken" the sacred texts to ourselves (2 Nephi 11:8) until we liken the concrete problems of the prophets' lives—their dilemmas and how they were delivered from them—to those we feel in our own lives. The more detail we know about who those ancient holy men and women were and what went on in their lives, the more perceptively we will be able to see how God's dealings with them can be applied to our relationship with him.

Geography, as much as history or culture, is an essential feature of life's problems. Many problems faced by the Nephite prophets and their people, and from which the hand of the Lord saved them so often, were shaped decisively by their geographical setting. To what degree did harsh physical conditions trigger the complaints of Lehi$_1$'s party in the Arabian desert (see 1 Nephi 16:19–20, 35–36)? What strategic concerns worried Captain Moroni about the rebellion and flight of Morianton (see Alma 50:30, 32)? Why were Moroni$_1$ and Pahoran$_1$ even more angry and concerned over the dissenters who seized power in the center of Nephite lands than they were over the powerful Lamanite armies on the periphery (see Alma 60–62)? How was geography central to the defeat of the robbers of Giddianhi (see 3 Nephi 3–4)? How many times did flight and relocation save Nephite groups from slavery or extinction (see, for example, Omni 1:12–13; Mosiah 24:17–21)? Geographical factors are pivotal in the Nephite experience. In fact, the title page of the Book of Mormon praises the "great things the Lord hath done for their fathers," and we can appreciate those "great things" so much better when we know of the places where they unfolded. Significantly, one of Nephi$_1$'s key teachings to his brothers was how the Lord uses geography to accomplish his ends (see 1 Nephi 17:23–26, 32–38).

Some may contend that we know enough about this topic already, but the actual extent of our knowledge is limited and unsystematized. Our copies of the Bible include a superb set of maps to which good teachers and wise students of the scripture turn frequently for clarification. After many years of doing without maps to inform us about key events and places mentioned in the Doctrine and Covenants, we finally received help in that regard starting with the 1981 edition of the scriptures. But our copies of the Book of Mormon still lack even the most basic map to clarify the complicated goings and comings reported in our keystone scripture. It appears that there is much yet to learn about the topic of Book of Mormon geography.

What is the status of the study of the geography in the Book of Mormon?

In the 170 years since the Book of Mormon was first published, its geography has been given comparatively little attention. Remarkably, what logically would seem to be one of the first steps in a systematic investigation—to construct a map of the American "land of promise" based solely on statements in that scripture (at least 550 passages are relevant)—seems not to have occurred to anyone during the church's first century. The first attempt appeared in print only in 1938.[3] In fact, a good deal of suspicion about and opposition to studying Book of Mormon geography has been manifested among Latter-day Saints, and this can in part be credited to the generally poor quality of the research and logic in previous investigations. The idea that as a church we have neglected the Book of Mormon[4] can apply to all aspects of the Book of Mormon, including geography.

A tiny minority of LDS (and RLDS) people have, nevertheless, been fascinated by the intellectual challenge and inspirational possibilities of a geography. At least eighty versions of a Book of Mormon map have been produced.[5] Most start with the writer confidently identifying some American area as the center where the Nephites lived and then distributing cities, lands, or other features named in the text to more or less agree with the original "solution." Ideas have ranged from identifying the promised land as the entire hemisphere to limiting the scene to a small portion of, say, Costa Rica or New York. Few of these writers have been knowledgeable about the range of elements that would go into a comprehensive and critical statement of the geography (such as language distributions, ecological zones, or archaeological finds). The result has been tremendous confusion and a plethora of notions that holds no promise of producing a consensus.

Didn't church leaders long ago settle the question of Nephite geography?

The simple answer to this question is no. Historical documents fail to indicate that church authorities have ever claimed that the lands of the Nephites were located in any particular place.

To explain more thoroughly, more than one view of where the Nephites lived was held in the early days of the church. It is possible to conclude that to the first readers of the Book of Mormon it seemed obvious that North America was the land northward and South America was the land southward, with the narrow neck of land at Panama. Because the angel Moroni first showed the plates to Joseph Smith at the hill near Joseph's home in New York State, church members supposed that the final battle between the Nephite and Lamanite armies occurred there too.[6] (Actually, what the account says is that while Mormon buried all the other records of the Nephite people in the hill Cumorah of the final battle, he gave the set of plates on which he had written his abridged history to his son Moroni$_2$ [see Mormon 6:6]. Moroni$_2$ still had those records in his possession thirty-five years later, after wandering "whithersoever I can" [Moroni 1:3] for safety from his enemies [see Mormon 8:4, 14; Moroni 10:1–2]. Moroni$_2$ did not tell us where he finally buried them. Perhaps the primary reason that he lived so long after the final battle was to deliver the plates to New York personally.)

In 1842, the church leaders in Nauvoo were presented with a newly published book[7] that spurred a new interpretation of Book of Mormon geography. A best-selling volume by explorer John Lloyd Stephens reported his dramatic discovery of great ruins in Central America, and it was reviewed enthusiastically in the *Times and Seasons*, Nauvoo's newspaper.[8] The author of the review is not known, but John Taylor was managing editor of the paper and Joseph Smith had declared six months before that "I alone stand responsible for it [the paper]."[9] The Nephites, the newspaper said, "lived about the narrow neck of land, which now embraces Central America." Furthermore, "the city of Zarahemla . . . stood upon this land." Of course, that would make the land southward, which included Zarahemla, a part of Central America ("several hundred miles of territory from north to south"),[10] not South America as had been thought.

Can this enthusiastic pronouncement be considered a revelation that defines the geography once and for all? No such claim was made. The active minds among the leaders were simply doing research. "We are not agoing to declare positively," the article said, "that the ruins of Quirigua [Guatemala] are those of Zarahemla, but when the land and the stones, and the books tell the story so plain, we are of opinion," that is, they inferred, that the site must be "one of those referred to in the Book of Mormon."[11] Additional comment in the next issue of the paper further reflects the intellectual ferment at work: "We have found another important fact." Clearly, they did not think that this new interpretation of the geography, or the original one, had settled matters, let alone been a revelation. They were doing what the Lord had instructed Oliver Cowdery to do in 1829: "You must study it out in your mind" (D&C 9:8). Apparently, they never reached a conclusion that satisfied everyone, because some of the leaders and most of the Saints, who were not privy to the thinking Stephens's book stirred among the small group around Joseph, continued to hold the two-continents interpretation.[12]

The fact that the geography question had not been settled authoritatively was confirmed by an 1890 statement from George Q. Cannon, counselor in the First Presidency: "The First Presidency have often been asked to prepare some suggestive map illustrative of Nephite geography, but have never consented to do so. Nor are we acquainted with any of the Twelve Apostles who would undertake such a task. The reason is, that without further information they are not prepared even to suggest [a map]. The word of the Lord or the translation of other ancient records is required to clear up many points now so obscure."[13] Around 1918 or a little before, church president Joseph F. Smith underlined the point. He "declined to officially approve of [any map], saying that the Lord had not yet revealed it."[14] By 1950 nothing had changed; apostle John A. Widtsoe said, "As far as can be learned, the Prophet Joseph Smith, translator of the book, did not say where, on the American continent, Book of Mormon activities occurred.

Perhaps he did not know. However, certain facts and traditions of varying reliability are used as foundation guides by students of Book of Mormon geography."[15]

No, the geography question has not been answered by church authorities, nor have the opinions worked out by geography hobbyists yet led to agreement. In 1947 it was still possible to hope that "out of the studies of faithful Latter-day Saints may yet come a unity of opinion concerning Book of Mormon geography," as Elder Widtsoe put it.[16] But in the half century since, confusion has grown. Few have sought consensus, while many have defensively adhered to individual notions based on selected "facts and traditions of varying reliability."

A different approach seems to be called for if we are to gain a better understanding of Book of Mormon geography and the benefits associated with that.

$\mathcal{H}$ow Can We Arrive at Mormon's Map?

To start at the beginning seems like a good plan in solving any problem. The beginning in addressing Book of Mormon geography is the text of the Book of Mormon itself. Elder Joseph Fielding Smith put the principle well for Latter-day Saints: "The teachings of any . . . member of the Church, high or low, if they do not square with the revelations, we need not accept them."[17] Whatever the Book of Mormon says about its own geography thus takes precedence over anything commentators have said of it.

The nearest thing to a systematic explanation of Mormon's geographical picture is given in Alma 22:27–34. In the course of relating an incident involving Nephite missionaries and the great king over the Lamanites, Mormon inserted a 570-word aside that summarized major features of the land southward. He must have considered that treatment full and clear enough for his purposes, because he never returned to the topic. Overall, over 550 verses in the Book of Mormon contain information of geographical significance: the account is steeped with information about the where of Nephite events. If we wish to learn what Mormon knew about the geography of his lands, we will have to flesh out the picture on our own, often by teasing the information out of the stories the ancient compiler presented.

When we examine the text, does a consistent geographical picture emerge?

Any story that is securely based on historical events demonstrates its genuineness by how consistently it refers to places. If an author or editor fails to have a specific setting in mind, discordant details will appear in statements about location, and inconsistencies in the fiction will become apparent. A large portion of the Book of Mormon was selected and phrased by just one man, Mormon, so the degree of consistency should be largely unmarred by the lapses of memory or slips of the pen (or stylus) that tend to accumulate in records handed down through multiple generations. My personal experience with the text of the Book of Mormon is that all the geographical information does prove to be consistent, so I conclude that Mormon possessed an orderly "mental map" of the scene on which his people's history was played out.[18]

We could wish for more detail than he gives us, but his information is still substantial. We both have the advantage of and are limited by what is found in the pages of the Book of Mormon. Some fifteen lands are named therein, and their positions are noted, connoted, or implied. The positions of forty-seven cities are more or less characterized (thirteen of these forty-seven are mentioned only once, and that limited data fails to provide enough information to relate the thirteen to the locations of other cities or lands). Mormon leaves no evidence of confusion about geography; he easily persuades me that he could have told us more had he chosen to do so. Even when particular lands or cities are mentioned at widely separated places in the text, the statements fit comfortably together into a plausible whole. He never hints that he did not understand the geography behind the records of his ancestors that he was abridging; rather, his writing exudes an air of confidence. That probably came in part from his own life experiences. According to his account (see Mormon), he personally traveled through much of the Nephite lands. In fact, he was a military leader and strategist who was accustomed to paying close attention to the lay of the land, and he may also have had actual maps to which he could refer.

Is there any reason why we should not try to reconstruct Mormon's map?

How could there be? The book that Mormon left us challenges us, its readers, to approach it with all our heart, might, mind, and strength. No one should object to more rigorous examination if through it we are able to discover new truth. We seek only the truth, and the truth will come out. We are not adding anything to the text, but simply combing it from a different point of view in order to exhaust what it has to tell us.

Still, some may argue that we cannot hope to attain clarity because of the great destruction that took place at the time of the Savior's crucifixion. They may feel that that event so changed everything that what could be seen of the landscape in former times would not be recognizable afterward. Mormon lets us know that this concern is unfounded. He prepared his record in the fourth century A.D., centuries after the famous natural catastrophe, yet he was not confused about geographical changes that had occurred at the meridian of time. Note the continuities: Zarahemla was destroyed but was soon rebuilt in the same spot (see 4 Nephi 1:8), next to the same river Sidon.

The Lamanites renewed warfare in Mormon's time in the same area of the upper Sidon where their predecessors hundreds of years earlier had typically attacked (compare Mormon 1:10; Alma 2:34; 3:20–23). The narrow pass was still the strategic access point for travelers going into the land northward, as much for Mormon's defending army around A.D. 350 as it had been in Morianton's day more than four hundred years before (compare Mormon 3:5; Alma 50:33–34). The Jaredite hill Ramah was called by the Nephites the hill Cumorah (see Ether 15:11), but it was exactly the same hill. Even at Bountiful, a few months after the vast storm and earthquake, while survivors were wondering at "the great and marvelous change which had taken place" in their surroundings (3 Nephi 11:1), their city and temple were still in place, their homes remained (see 3 Nephi 19:1), they obviously had a continuing food supply, and their communication networks were still in place (see 3 Nephi 19:2–3). The catastrophe had changed the "face of the land" (3 Nephi 8:12), but a changed face apparently did not mean that most of the basic land forms and ecological conditions had been rendered unrecognizable.

In any case, the test is in the doing. If we find that the Nephite record permits us to make a map that works both before and after the crucifixion, then we can be assured that the giant destruction does not make it necessary to picture one pattern of geography before and a very different one afterward. We will see that this is so.

How might we proceed to discover the map in Mormon's mind?

We must, as indicated earlier, intensively examine the text Mormon left us (of course, we have access to it only as it has been transmitted to us in English through Joseph Smith). We must discover as many of the geographical clues he included as we can. But before we undertake that task, we need to spell out some assumptions that will undergird our search through his record:

1. The expressions "up," "down," and "over," when used in a geographical context, refer to elevation. (It turns out that they are used consistently and make sense in terms of elevation.)

2. Nature worked the same anciently as it does today. For example, we can be sure that the headwaters of rivers were at a higher elevation than their mouths, and a river implies the presence of a corresponding drainage basin. (This may seem too obvious to deserve mentioning; however, some students of Book of Mormon geography seem to have missed the point.)

3. Ideas in the record will not necessarily be familiar or clear to us. There was some degree of continuity in Nephite thought and expression from the Hebrew/Israelite roots of Lehi$_1$'s time, but it was only partial. Mormon could read and compile from his people's archive of traditional records, so his patterns of thought and terminology still followed with sufficient continuity from his predecessors that he was part of a continuous scribal tradition passed down through the preceding nine centuries. That tradition may have required special training to master the old script and records.

4. Book of Mormon terminology will not necessarily be clear to us, even in translation, because language and cultural assumptions change. According to Moroni$_2$ in Mormon 9:34, major changes in language occurred over the Nephite generations, for "none other people knoweth our language." Furthermore, English has changed between 1829

and 2000. We must seek to overcome any problems this causes us by striving to think, feel, and see as if we were Mormon, rather than supposing that we can read the text "literally" (which actually turns out to mean "according to unspoken assumptions of our current culture").

5. Finally, when we are combining fragments of geographical information from the text into sensible wholes, we should avoid needlessly complicated synthesis. If two explanations occur to us for solving a geographical problem, the simpler solution—the one with the fewest arbitrary assumptions— is probably better. For example, we should resist the temptation to suppose that there were two cities with the same name simply because we have not yet determined how the correct placement of a single city would resolve any apparent confusion.

Now we are ready to begin poring over the Book of Mormon text to glean all the geographical information we can. If we are fortunate enough to accommodate every statement in the text into one geographical model, then our map can be considered definitive: we can then assume that we have discovered and reconstructed Mormon's map. If we are still left with some uncertainties that we cannot manage logically, then we will just have to settle for the optimal solution, the one that leaves us with the least number of the book's statements rationally unaccounted for.

Our search will be simplified if we split up the problem into separate tasks. The remaining chapters in this book divide the labor into six segments. Each segment is discussed in a chapter that lays out key passages from the Book of Mormon that shed light on topics like these:

- The overall configuration of the lands
- Topography (land surfaces) and hydrography (streams, lakes, and seas)
- Distances and directions
- Climate, ecology, economy, and population
- The distribution of the civilization
- Nephite history in geographical perspective

It is impossible in this short treatment to deal with all the scriptural passages that contain information about this subject. Besides, a nearly exhaustive analysis has already been published.[19] Here we will review mainly the most decisive and clearest statements. A series of questions will be used to frame subtopics.

chapter 3

*T*he Overall Configuration

In this and succeeding chapters it is important to keep in mind that we are trying to detect the Nephites' *conception* of their geography, not to identify actual physical settings that lay behind their ideas. We have no way to recover information on their real-world setting from the book; all we can hope to learn is what Mormon and those of his predecessors from whom he quotes "knew." Because the Book of Mormon writers processed information about their piece of the world through cultural lenses, we must carefully analyze their geographical statements and their implications in order to fully understand them. We will need to discern the geographical data they reveal in their statements, like a person who learns a foreign language by piecing together the tongue by listening alertly and repeatedly to what native speakers say. After much practice in the new language, patterns become second nature. The map that the Nephites used may seem odd to us, like a new language. Another people's conceptions of geography may be distorted by the participant's interests, experiences, and traditions: a Nephite might have cared little and known less about Lamanite territory in the land of Nephi but would have controlled a lot of detail about his own land of Zarahemla. (Consider those humorous maps of the United States "according to a New Yorker," in which the territory west of the Hudson River fades off quickly into a vague "West" that consists of little more than Chicago, Las Vegas, and Hollywood.) Our task will be to sift through the words left to us by Nephite writers in order to reconstruct the mental geography they shared.

What was the overall shape of Nephite and Lamanite lands?

We should begin with the clearest and fullest information in the Book of Mormon text, which comes from Alma 22:32. Mormon explained that "the land of Nephi and the land of Zarahemla," a combined unit constituting almost the entire land southward, "were nearly surrounded by water." This agrees with the statement in 2 Nephi 10:20: "We are upon an isle of the sea." (In the King James Version of the Bible and generally in the Book of Mormon, an "isle" was not necessarily completely surrounded by water; it was simply a place to which routine access was by sea, even though a traveler might reach it by a land route as well.)[20] There was "a small neck of land between the land northward and the land southward" that "was only the distance of a day and a half's journey for a Nephite, on the line [that marked the boundary between] Bountiful and the land Desolation, from the east to the west sea." The basic shape of the two lands and isthmus are seen on map 1.

No specific information is provided about the shape or extent of the land northward, but we can conclude from its being paired with the land southward (as in Helaman 6:10) that it expanded from the narrow neck to be roughly comparable in scale to the land southward. (See the next chapter for more on the land northward.)

The directional trend of the two lands and the neck was

MAP 1. OVERALL SHAPE

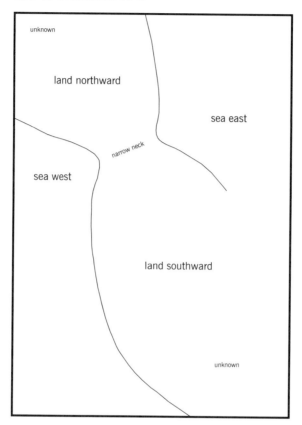

The fundamental geographical configuration of the "promised land" was like an hourglass, with the land southward "nearly surrounded by water" (Alma 22:32).

generally north-south. The east sea (six references) and the west sea (twelve references) were the primary bodies of water that bounded this promised land. But notice that the key term of reference is not "land north" (only five references) but "land northward" (thirty-one references). There is, of course, a distinction; "land northward" implies a direction somewhat off from literal north. This implication that the lands are not simply oriented to the cardinal directions is confirmed by reference to the "sea north" and "sea south" (Helaman 3:8). These terms are used only once, in reference to the colonizing of the land northward by the Nephites, but not in connection with the land southward. The only way to have seas north and south on a literal or descriptive basis would be for the two major bodies of land to be oriented at an angle somewhat off true north-south. That would allow part of the ocean to lie toward the south of one and another part of the ocean to lie toward north of the other.

What was the nature of the "narrow neck of land"?

An isthmus, "the place where the sea divides the land" (Ether 10:20), connected the two major blocks of land. Alma 22:32 pictures "the land northward and the land southward" joined by "a small neck of land between." In Alma 63:5 and elsewhere it is labeled the "narrow neck." This isthmus had sea to the west and to the east (see Alma 50:34; 63:5; Helaman 4:7). These seas had to be the Pacific and Atlantic oceans, respectively, because Lehi₁ arrived from the Old World across the west sea (see Alma 22:28), and the party that brought Mulek from the land of Judah came "across the great waters" (Omni 1:16) to the "borders by the east sea." The city of Mulek was located in that area and was presumably near the location where they first settled (see Alma 51:26).[21]

Because there were oceans on either side of the isthmus, a continental divide passed through it along its northward-southward axis. The land of Bountiful stretched across the isthmus. Its chief city, Bountiful, was virtually at sea level (shown by the adjacent beach reported in Alma 51:28, 32), which suggests that the entire isthmus was relatively low-lying as well.

How wide was this narrow neck? One historical anecdote makes clear that it was wide enough that a party passing through it could not detect seas on either side. Limhi's explorers traveled northward from the land of Nephi trying to locate Zarahemla but wandered on through the narrow neck. When they returned home they thought they had been in the land southward the whole time. Actually, they had journeyed all the way through the neck to the zone of the Jaredites' final battles (see Mosiah 8:8; 21:25). (Had there been any mountain near their route, they might have climbed it to reconnoiter, seen the sea, and reevaluated their position.) Later, however, after further exploration, the Nephites came to realize that the neck connected two major land masses. Still later, in the fourth century A.D. when Mormon prepared his account of Nephite history, it was well-known among his people that it was "the distance of a day and a half's journey for a Nephite" across the isthmus (Alma 22:32). (See chapter 5 for what that statement might signify in terms of miles.)

Within the neck was what can only have been a specific geological structure called the "narrow pass" or "narrow passage" (Alma 50:34; 52:9; Mormon 2:29). It lay toward the east side of the isthmus, not in the center (see Alma 51:30, 32; 52:9).[22] This feature was so focused and localized that the Nephite military leader Teancum positioned his army at the entrance to the pass, which was precisely the point where he knew fugitive Morianton and his people would head in order to get to the land northward (see Alma 50:34–35). No other route existed that allowed passage for a large group into the easterly side of the land northward, which is where the mass of Nephite colonists in the land northward apparently located. By holding this narrow pass, later Nephite forces could keep the Lamanites from getting "possession of *any*" of the Nephites' lands northward (see Mormon 3:5–6). Subsequent events showed that those lands were exclusively on the eastern side.

Did the lands northward and southward together constitute the entire "promised land"?

Yes, in terms of Nephite thinking. Nephi₁ reported that his party "did arrive at the promised land" and "did call it the promised land" (1 Nephi 18:23). This landing point was in the land southward, "on the west in the land of Nephi, in the place of their fathers' first inheritance . . . by the seashore" (Alma 22:28). But the Jaredites "did land upon the shore of the promised land" (Ether 6:12) in the land northward (see Ether 10:21).

That the two lands were conceived by the Nephites as a single "promised land" is underlined by the words of Captain Moroni, when he "named all the land which was south of the land Desolation, yea, and in fine, all the land, both on the north and on the south—A chosen land, and the land of liberty" (Alma 46:17).²³ The essential unity of the combined territory was reemphasized by events occurring shortly before the crucifixion of the Savior. Third Nephi 3 tells of the grave threat robber groups posed to the consolidated society of the righteous Nephites and Lamanites. The problem became so great that Lachoneus, the leader of the defenders, ordered his people to assemble "together their women, and their children, their flocks and their herds, and all their substance, save it were their land, unto one place" (3 Nephi 3:13). The proclamation to gather "had gone forth throughout all the face of the land," directing the beleaguered believers to dwell "in one land and in one body" (3 Nephi 3:22, 25). The designated refuge zone proved to be small enough that enemy forces could surround and besiege it (see 3 Nephi 4:16). To that appointed spot in the northern portion of the land southward all the Nephites and their Lamanite supporters gathered from all parts of the land southward as well as from the colonies in the land northward (see 3 Nephi 3:23–24). Later, when the situation was resolved, these people "did return to their own lands and their possessions, both on the north and on the south, both on the land northward and on the land southward" (3 Nephi 6:2). This all makes sense only if they were talking about a unified settled territory, partly south of the narrow neck and partly to the north. Further confirmation that they considered the domain designated as "the promised land" to be relatively compact, continuous, and complete in itself comes from the finality and brevity of the statement in Helaman 6:10: "Now the land south was called Lehi, and the land north was called Mulek." The preceding verses connote that when the Nephites referred to these paired lands, they meant nothing was left over—at least nothing that interested them.

The possibility exists that they knew of other lands but simply did not consider them relevant. For example, Nephites extensively colonized the land northward (see Alma 63:4, 9; Helaman 3:3–12), even to include part of the west sea coast. Yet the final military movements in the Nephites' last decades occurred in an area within a limited distance of the narrow pass—the specific city and land of Desolation and lands nearby, including Cumorah, all of which were located toward the east sea side of the land northward. Nothing in Mormon's account suggests any "ups" or "downs" within the Nephite land northward. The area of the Jaredite settlements and wars, on the other hand, encompassed major changes in elevation between the land of Moron and the more easterly areas of the land northward. It seems that the Nephites were simply not concerned with the uplands of the land northward, although they surely knew of their existence.

The Nephites' interest was selective, we know. Take the case of the shipbuilder Hagoth. He provides an interesting footnote, but his colonization of the west coast of the land northward had little or no effect on Nephite history. Only four ships are actually mentioned, and the fate of two of those is left doubtful (see Alma 63:5–10), as is the fate of the colonists they bore northward. After heading by sea to the new colony to the north, Alma$_2$'s son Corianton seems not to have been heard from again, and Mormon's account of the final Nephite decades omits any information about involvement of west-coast folks with the main body of Nephites. The possibility thus exists that some territories connected with what the Nephites conceived as the promised land proved neither interesting nor significant to the main history of that people. (Just as, for example, the history of Israel as recorded in the Old Testament ignores nearly all events in such close-at-hand areas as Arabia, Sinai, and Syria.)

If the Nephite writers knew of connecting lands northward or southward beyond what they considered the Nephite promised land, we have only ambiguous indication of the fact. Lehi$_1$'s blessing on his sons warned that "this land" would be kept "as yet" from a knowledge of other nations, but "when the time cometh that they shall dwindle in unbelief," the Lord would "bring other nations unto them" (2 Nephi 1:8, 10, 11). That sounds as if other groups were just off stage but would show up no later than when the Nephites were exterminated. The Jaredite prophet Ether knew "concerning a New Jerusalem [to be built] upon this land" (Ether 13:4; see 13:6, 8), which we interpret these days to refer to North America, but he did not relate the area he envisioned to events among his own people or the Nephites. The Savior prophesied of the same future city "in this land" (3 Nephi 20:22), although the great destruction of cities his voice proclaimed in 3 Nephi 9 can be identified as occurring in the lands southward or northward or else are plausibly associated with them. (But at least some of the Nephite prophets seem to have understood that the original promised land, and its promises, could be extended to encompass more distant territory, probably in the same manner as we use "America" to refer not only to the United States but also to North and South America together).

Mormon's expression in Alma 22:32 about the land southward being "nearly" surrounded by water leaves the possibility open that southward from the Lamanites and northward from the Nephite zones, connecting lands existed, even though they might not be discussed in the history contained in Mormon's record. The record mentions no specific lands or cities that lay southward beyond the land of Nephi or the land of first inheritance. At the northerly extremity of Nephite holdings, relationships are also left vague. Dissidents under a man named Jacob at one time fled to "the northernmost part of the land" (3 Nephi 7:12). They would not have gone far, however, for their intention was to accumulate strength there in order to return and seize control of the main Nephite lands from which they had fled. Moreover, when the voice of the Lord announced that Jacob$_4$'s city, Jacobugath, had been destroyed in the great catastrophe, it was listed as simply one among the cities destroyed in the overall promised land, not as though it lay at some great distance. While the possibility cannot be ruled out that land stretched farther north than "the northernmost part," we must suppose that whatever was there was of no interest to the Nephite historians or was beyond the range of their knowledge. Thus on both the north and south extremities, we end up marking any reconstructed Nephite map "unknown."

Where were the major ethnic, social, or political groups based in the promised land?

Shortly before their demise, the Nephites were driven entirely out of the land southward (see Mormon 2:29), but in preceding centuries their heartland had been the northern part of that land. Mormon summarized their distribution in the crucial and most fully reported middle era (see Alma 22:27–29, 33–34). The Lamanite king's domain stretched from the capital city, Lehi-Nephi, "even to the sea, on the east and on the west." The main block of this territory lay southward of Nephite holdings, although some Lamanites "were spread through the wilderness on the west, in the land of Nephi" from "the place of their fathers' first inheritance" northward along the west coast of the land of Zarahemla "even until they came to the land . . . Bountiful." That extension along the west sea coast was matched on the east sea side of the land of Zarahemla; there, we are told, Lamanites inhabited a strip of wilderness that extended northward along the coast as far as the land Bountiful. Thus at this point in time the Nephite land of Zarahemla was surrounded on three sides by Lamanites. (See map 2.) But under Captain Moroni in the early part of the last century B.C., the Nephites expelled the Lamanite squatters along both coasts, driving them southward into the land of Nephi proper that was the traditional Lamanite possession (see Alma 50:7–11).

The main Nephite stronghold in the center of the land along the river Sidon was separated from the Lamanites by "a narrow strip of wilderness" (Alma 22:27); it was composed of rugged mountains within which lay the headwaters of the river Sidon. The Nephites sat in the land of Zarahemla, just northward from that transverse strip of wilderness and southward from the narrow neck, like a cork in a bottle. The expansionist

MAP 2. CHIEF ETHNIC AREAS

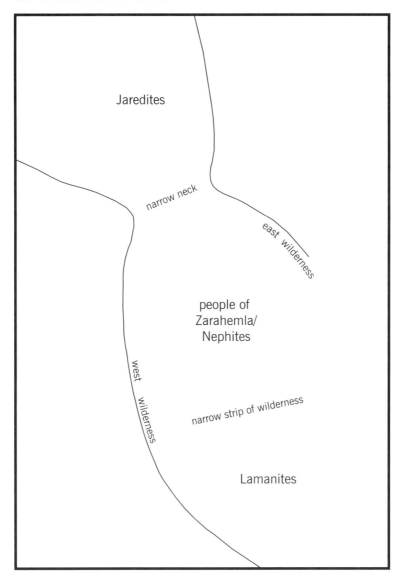

At the time when Mormon's text gives us the most detailed information, the Lamanites were located in the land of Nephi. The people of Zarahemla (sometimes called the Mulekites) were ruled by the Nephites in the north portion of the land southward. The Jaredites were extinct by Mosiah$_1$'s day.

Lamanite rulers kept up pressure on them from the south, but the Nephite defenders held them off for a long time by inhabiting "the land Bountiful [and Zarahemla], even from the east unto the west sea . . . that thereby [the Lamanites] should have no more possession on the north" of what they then held. Nephite strategy was to keep their enemies "hemmed in" so that "they might not overrun the land northward" (Alma 22:33). The Nephites wanted to be able, if worst came to worst, to "have a country [the land northward] whither they might flee" (Alma 22:34). Conversely, the Lamanite leaders were obsessed with finding a way to pop the cork and gain access to the land northward in order to surround their traditional enemies completely and thus "have power to harass them on every side" (Alma 52:9). The Lamanite-Nephite wars, which went on for centuries, from Benjamin's day (see Omni 1:24) to Mormon's (see Mormon 5), turned on the key geographical fact that the Nephites held a relatively secure position in their Zarahemla heartland as long as they could blunt the Lamanite probes and keep them from reaching the neck. Amalickiah was almost successful on the east coast, getting within a few miles of the land northward (see Alma 52:27–28). Coriantumr$_2$ led a disastrous Lamanite assault through the middle of the land of Zarahemla, which proved that this route merely played to Nephite strength (see Helaman 1:18, 22–27; compare Alma 60:19). Lamanite armed excursions along the west sea coast were no more successful in reaching the coveted isthmus (see Alma 16:2; 49:1–9).

If the explanation of the keys to Nephite geography seems thus far cast in unduly military terms, keep in mind that our account comes through Mormon, a military commander and strategist through all his adult life. He saw clearly that the problems faced by Captain Moroni and other earlier Nephite commanders in protecting their people against the Lamanite invaders were essentially the same as those that faced him four centuries later. The strategic geography had not changed over the generations, and the problems it posed were in the forefront of his thinking all his life. Mormon's mental map of the promised land was a military one, so as we reconstruct it we must frequently refer to the intricate Nephite-Lamanite military history.

Where were the Jaredites located?

The Jaredites' major settlement area was the land northward (see Ether 10:20–21). From shortly after their landing on the coast (whether they came by the east sea or the west sea is not clear, but the latter seems somewhat more likely), their political center was the land of Moron, and it remained crucial until the end of their history (see Ether 7:5–6, 11; 12:1; 14:6, 11). Moroni$_2$ reports that the land of Moron was in the land northward "near" (Ether 7:6) the land that the Nephites called Desolation. The final Jaredite wars were fought in the same Cumorah area as the final Nephite battle (see Ether 9:3). We are also told that the Jaredites built a great city at the narrow neck of land, yet they did not (at least not specifically) settle in the land southward (see Ether 10:20; see also 9:31–35).

Where did the Mulekites settle?

The city of Mulek was in the borders by the east sea. We can suppose that this was one of the Mulekites' earliest settlements (note that the Nephites named cities after their original founder, and the Mulekites probably did the same; see Alma 8:7). Further, the Mulek group discovered the final Jaredite ruler, Coriantumr$_1$, shortly after the Jaredites' final struggle, and that had to have taken place near the east sea (see Omni 1:21; Ether 9:3). The Mulek party is reported to have first arrived in the land northward (see Helaman 6:10), then some of their descendants "came from there up" to where the Nephites found them, in and around the city of Zarahemla on the upper Sidon River (Alma 22:30–31; see Helaman 6:10).

Summary

The Nephites, including Mormon, conceived of the lands of concern to them as centered in the isthmian zone that connected two larger territories, the land northward and the land southward. The land southward was "nearly surrounded" (Alma 22:32) by ocean waters, and the land northward was also bounded by oceans; the original immigrant parties arrived from the Old World across these waters. The Nephite writers did not see their land of promise as merely a segment within and surrounded by a continental land mass, and we shall establish later that the dimensions of their geographical picture were far smaller than those of any continent.

While all details of the configuration of lands cannot be settled definitively from the statements we have available, what is said fits together consistently if we consider the basic shape of the lands to be rather like an hourglass.

chapter 4
*T*he Surface of the Land

Each time we seek to discover what the Book of Mormon says on a new topic, we essentially have to comb the whole text anew, because it is not possible for a person to focus on many objectives at one time. Now that we have established the broad configuration of Nephite lands in chapter 3, we will next examine what the account tells us concerning topography—the relative elevations of portions of the land—and the closely associated data on bodies of water and streams.

Since the Book of Mormon account is historical, its geographical data come from different periods of time. The Nephites' mental map would have changed somewhat—matured or filled in—over time. The notions held by Nephi$_1$ and his brother Jacob in the sixth century B.C. would have been limited and incomplete compared with the geographical knowledge of Alma$_2$ centuries later. Mormon, of course, could draw on all the Nephite records from the past, and his own extensive travels gave him unparalleled firsthand knowledge of geography. Because Mormon is the source of most of the language in the record as we have it, we can suppose he resolved any geographical

inconsistencies that were due to lack of knowledge on the part
of earlier writers. (We wish that Moroni$_2$ had done as much for
us in regard to the geography of the book of Ether, but he left
many questions unanswered in his brief treatment.)

When we read the record, we must keep in mind that some
terminology changed over time. The land of Zarahemla, for
example, is not the same area throughout the Book of Mormon.
In the book of Omni, the name was applied only to a local area
around the city of Zarahemla (see 1:13; Mosiah 1:10; 2:1). By
the time Alma$_2$ made his missionary circuit to Gideon, Melek,
Ammonihah, and Sidom, a major part of the Sidon River basin
was included in the land of Zarahemla, and a little later the
borders by the east sea also came under the umbrella term
"land of Zarahemla" (see Alma 50:7, 11).

**What were the main variations in elevation in the land
southward?**

The land of Zarahemla was well above sea level; Mormon's
basic sketch of the geography says that from the first landing
place of the people of Zarahemla, which would have been at
sea level, "they came from there up into the south wilderness"
(Alma 22:30–31), where Mosiah$_1$ found them (see Omni
1:13–14). That is a fairly obvious but little noted point; the
river Sidon at the city of Zarahemla was not far distant from its
headwaters, so it still had a long way to flow—downhill—
before it reached the sea (see Alma 22:27; 50:11; 56:25).

When we compare what the record says about the two major segments of the land southward, a major topographic contrast comes to light. The Nephite possessions in the land of
Zarahemla are distinctly and consistently said to be lower in
elevation than Lamanite-occupied highland Nephi. The book

of Omni first shows this when it reports the Nephites' discovery of the people of Zarahemla: "Mosiah, . . . being warned of the Lord that he should flee out of the land of Nephi, and as many as would hearken unto the voice of the Lord . . . , came down into the land which is called the land of Zarahemla" (1:12–13). Shortly after, "a certain number . . . went up into the wilderness to return to the land of Nephi" (Omni 1:27). This relationship is reaffirmed dozens of times. (The pattern of referring to topography in terms of "up" and "down" had, of course, been manifested from the beginning of Nephi$_1$'s record; his family went "down" from the Jerusalem area to near the shores of the Red Sea [1 Nephi 2:5], and he and his brothers later returned "up" to Jerusalem [1 Nephi 3:9].)

The difference in elevation between the two major territorial divisions—Zarahemla of the Nephites and Nephi of the Lamanites—is again shown in the account of a party who went to the land of Nephi to find out what had happened to the people of Zeniff. Zeniff's group had been gone for decades, and now the search party "knew not the course they should travel in the wilderness to go up . . . therefore they wandered many days in the wilderness" (Mosiah 7:4). The sons of Mosiah$_2$ and their companions faced similar hardship traversing the same route (see Alma 17:5–8). The abrupt topographic contrast travelers faced led the Nephite writers to use the specific expression "narrow strip of wilderness" (Alma 22:27) to label this transitional stretch. The "head [waters] of the river Sidon" lay within this rugged mountain band (Alma 22:29; 43:22).

The primary land of Nephi was also consistently "up" in relation to the seas on either side. The east sea formed one boundary for the general land of Nephi (see Alma 22:27). From the Lamanite capital, the city of Nephi, the Lamanite army came down to attack the city of Moroni beside the east sea (see Alma 51:11, 22). On the western side of the land of Nephi a progression of lands staircased from the coast upward: from the Lamanite king's unnamed homeland near the sea, to Shemlon, to Shilom, and then to the local land of Nephi (see Mosiah 20:7, 9; 24:1–2). Highland Nephi remained the Lamanite base from which they launched most of their attacks on the Nephites from the days of King Benjamin (see Omni 1:24) to the time of Mormon five hundred years later (see Mormon 1:10; 3:7). Naturally enough, the topography of the uplands of the land of Nephi was broken. Alma$_1$ and his party were able to escape discovery for a number of years in a mountain valley that they called the land of Helam. Eventually they were discovered by an army of Lamanite soldiers who could not find their way back to their base at the city of Nephi. Wandering about, these lost Lamanites accidentally stumbled on two isolated peoples: the Amulonites, who also did not know how to get to Nephi, and then Alma$_1$'s folks.

A strip of wilderness paralleled the west sea coast all the way from the land of first inheritance on the southerly extremity, where Lehi$_1$ and his family first landed, to near the narrow neck (see Alma 22:28–29). Forested coastal lowlands as well as a mountain range must have constituted that wilderness. That area was apparently not occupied by Nephites, for the record tells of no settlements there. They considered it occupied only by barbaric Lamanites who had filtered up from the south, and even when the Lamanites living there were eliminated (see Alma 50:11), the Nephites failed to settle that western strip seriously until near the end of their history. The text names no Nephite lands there until Mormon's day, when the retreating Nephites occupied a land called Joshua at the northerly end of the west strip (see Mormon 2:6).

What are the distinguishing features of the topography of the land of Zarahemla?

Just inland from the west coastal strip rose a mountain chain that formed the west side of the basin of the one major river talked about in the Book of Mormon, the Sidon. That basin was a major feature of the landscape in the land southward. The river's headwaters, as we have seen, were up in the rugged mountains that separated the lands of Zarahemla and Nephi.

The east side of the river basin was formed by elevated lands of which the mountain valley or land of Gideon was part (see Alma 2:17–20; 6:7). The rise on the east side of the river was quite abrupt; according to Alma 2:15, the river Sidon ran "by," not through, the land of Zarahemla, implying that most of the Nephite settlements were west of the river. No named cities are mentioned on the east side of the Sidon within the land of Zarahemla proper except for Gideon. This picture of higher land lying close on the east side of the river is also suggested by Alma 15:18. From the land of Sidom (which was likely on the river, given the similarity of the names Sidom and Sidon, plus the emphasis on baptizing there), Alma$_2$ and Amulek ended their preaching and "came over to the [local] land of Zarahemla." Since there is no hint elsewhere in the text of an elevation between Sidom and Zarahemla that would account for the use of "over" if their route had been along or west of the river, it appears that they climbed up from the river, passed through the eastern upland, and then descended to reach the city of Zarahemla. Farther upstream the same situation of traveling southward over an elevation east of the river can be seen. Both the cities of Zarahemla and Manti lay beside the Sidon River, yet the regular route between the two detoured through the mountain valley of Gideon, as shown by Mosiah

22:11, 13; Alma 17:1; 27:16.[24] Moreover, from the land of Zarahemla a person "went" over (Alma 30:19; traveling the opposite
direction a person "came" over, 35:13) an intervening elevation
to reach Jershon in the lowland borders by the east sea; logically the elevation that was surmounted would have constituted the easterly side of the Sidon basin. These journeyings
and the silence of the record about Nephite settlements on the
east of the river confirm that the Sidon basin closed in directly
on the east side of the stream.

On the west side of the river Sidon there was more open
space. For example, to go westward from Zarahemla to the
land of Melek, Alma$_2$ took "his journey over into" the latter
land (see Alma 8:3–5). This sounds like a more involved trip
than going to Gideon on the east side, which was no more than
a day distant (see Alma 6:7; see also 2:15–20). Also on the west,
adjacent to the wilderness that bounded the land of Zarahemla
on the west, were the cities of Ammonihah and Noah (see
Alma 8:6; 15:1; 49:12). Judea and the southwest frontier cities
of Cumeni, Zeezrom, and Antiparah (see Alma 56:13–14, 25,
31) were also west of the big river, in the southwestern quad-
rant of the land of Zarahemla. Clearly, most of the territory the
Nephites had settled in the land of Zarahemla lay west of the
Sidon River.

When we realize that a river basin formed the core of the
land of Zarahemla, a number of other statements in Mormon's
record become clear. For instance, the people of Ammon,
whom the Lamanites wanted to destroy, were placed in the
land of Melek so that they would need no special military protection. Evidently, the Nephites considered that spot to offer
maximum safety from enemy attack (see Alma 35:10–13). Why
so? It was located "on the west of the river Sidon, on the west
by the borders of the wilderness" (Alma 8:3). Twice Lamanite

armies passed northward along the west coast wilderness strip, undetected and unopposed by Nephite forces, it seems. Both times they came "in upon the wilderness side" (Alma 16:2; see 49:1, 12) to target the city of Ammonihah, crossing "over" (Alma 25:2) the western edge of the Sidon basin from the west sea coast. Why did the Lamanites not cross "over" to attack the hated, undefended people of Ammon in Melek, three days' journey to the south of Ammonihah (see Alma 8:6)? The only evident reason is that the west wilderness was such a difficult barrier in the Melek area that the Lamanites did not consider an attack feasible. The mountains forming the western edge of the basin must have constituted a high, wide barrier through which there was no practical access near Melek.

We learn of two crossing points—mountain passes—between the west sea and the interior land of Zarahemla: (1) the one near Ammonihah, which the Lamanites twice sneaked through without being detected (the Nephites must have considered an attack there so unlikely that it did not occur to them to keep a regular watch), and (2) an access in the extreme southwestern quarter of the land. At this second point Helaman$_1$ and his 2060 young warriors lured the Lamanites out of the fortress city of Antiparah by appearing to skirt it "as if we were going to the city beyond, in the borders by the seashore" (Alma 56:31). Helaman$_1$'s men had come southward from their homeland in Melek to reinforce Judea, then had ascended past the cities of Zeezrom and Cumeni to reach Antiparah, the westernmost outpost held at that moment by the Lamanites (and apparently sited at or near the summit). Immediately westward lay the southern pass, from which the route descended to the city by the seashore (see Alma 56:31–32). Nowhere between this southern pass and the one near Ammonihah does there appear to have been any other established route through the

mountain chain. The Ammonites in Melek were thus in a per-
fectly secure position behind the western mountain rampart.
All this must have been so plain to Mormon that he saw no
point in giving his readers further geographical explanation
about the basin's obvious structure.

The existence of a pass into the basin near the city of
Ammonihah explains another historical situation. During
their final retreat under the command of young Mormon, the
Nephites were unable to find any strategic position within the
relatively open land of Zarahemla to block their Lamanite as-
sailants (see Mormon 2:2–5). They gained an advantage, however, when they moved out of the basin into "the land of Joshua,
which was in the borders west by the seashore" (Mormon 2:6).
Joshua was on the seaward side of the mountain pass the
Lamanites had gone "over" centuries before. At this point the
Nephites were able to hold the Lamanite armies back for four-
teen years. The reason quite surely was that the Lamanites were
unable to break out of the newly conquered land of Zarahemla,
the Sidon basin, through the heavily defended pass to get at the
main body of Nephites in Joshua down in the coastal borders.

Finally, when we appreciate the fact that the relatively isolated and defensible Sidon basin formed the Nephite homeland, Captain Moroni's angry words to Pahoran$_1$ make sense.
Moroni$_1$'s armies had been fighting a bruising war along the
east coast of the Nephite domain while Helaman$_2$'s armies had
been repelling the enemy threat in the southwest. Commander
in chief Moroni$_1$ wrote a harsh letter to the chief judge,
Pahoran$_1$, demanding support for the war effort out on the actual battle fronts. Among his charges he wrote, "Is it that ye
have neglected us because ye are in the heart of our country
and ye are surrounded by security?" (Alma 60:19). We have
seen that the people in the capital city indeed had reasons—

geographical reasons—for supposing that they were secure in their basin stronghold.

For a comprehensive view of the topography see the map Physical Features on the inside back cover of the book.

How did "the borders by the east sea" relate to the land of Zarahemla?

The most attractive route for the Lamanites who aimed to capture the narrow neck lay along the east sea coast. (We shall see in a later chapter that the shortest distance for them to traverse was along the east sea.) What is said about the military action in that sector contributes to our knowledge of the topography. Not long after Moroni$_1$ became the Nephites' military commander (see Alma 43:16–17), he was so concerned about the vulnerability of this area that he "caused that his armies should go forth into the east wilderness . . . and [they] drove all the Lamanites who were in the east wilderness into their own lands, which were south of the land of Zarahemla" (Alma 50:7). One reason for Moroni$_1$'s concern had to have been that this coastal area was wide enough that it was hard to defend against a northward Lamanite attack that would ultimately target the narrow neck. Moroni$_1$ sent settlers to settle, farm, and garrison the area that had just been cleared of Lamanite squatters, and as part of this effort, he constructed a series of fortified "instant cities." He also installed fortifications farther south, along a "line between the Nephites and the Lamanites" (see Alma 50:9–11). Clearly, he was dealing with a sizable territory that was quite unlike the narrow pass at the neck, where defenders could easily focus on an area small enough to allow them to intercept an attack (see Alma 50:34). Sure enough, when Amalickiah's Lamanite army did attack (see Alma 51:22–26), they had enough maneuvering options to break through Moroni₁'s defense scheme. The coastal plain was sufficiently wide that the Lamanite army could drive forward "down by the seashore" while bypassing Nephite strong points farther inland: Moroni₁'s base camp and the city of Jershon, and perhaps the city of Nephihah (see Alma 51:25).[25] Amalickiah's attack route can be seen on map 3.

MAP 3. AMALICKIAH'S ATTACK BY THE EAST SEASHORE

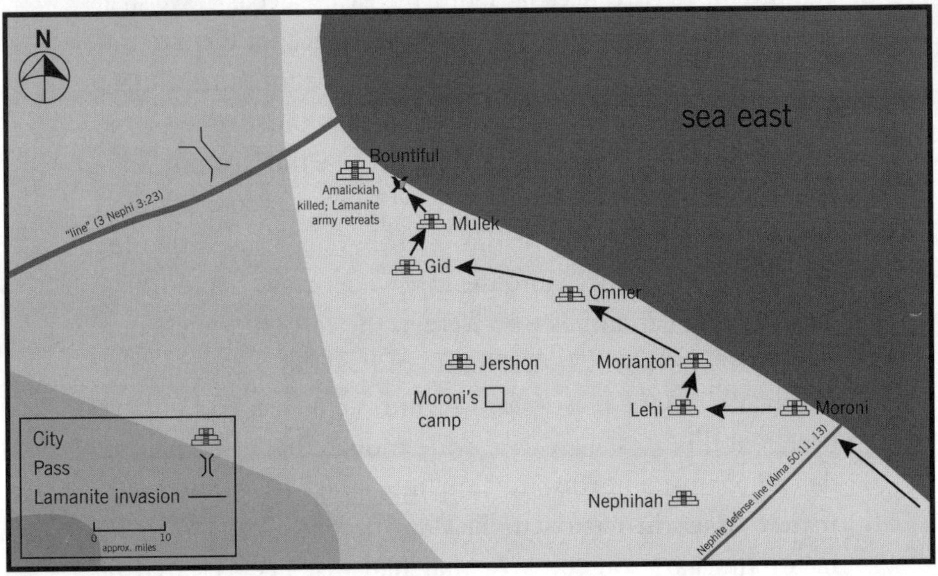

The Lamanite army's lightning strike stayed "down by the seashore" (Alma 51:25), leaving an inland strip containing the lands of Nephihah and Jershon in Nephite hands.

The width of this coastal territory is made clear in another incident, the flight of Morianton and Teancum's pursuit of him (see Alma 50:33–35). The accounts of Moroni₁'s defenses and Teancum's pursuit agree that at least two bands of settlements and trails paralleled the shoreline. Morianton's group followed a route toward the narrow pass nearer the coast, only to discover that Teancum's force had beaten them to their destination by going a wholly different way. The geography of the Morianton incident is shown on map 4.

MAP 4. TEANCUM INTERCEPTS MORIANTON

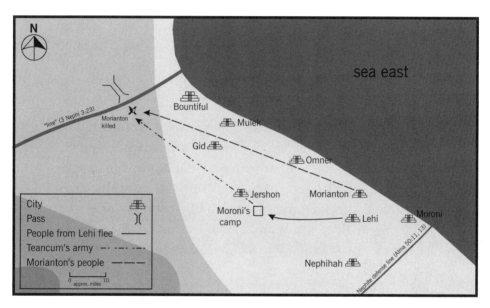

Rebellious Morianton and his group tried to flee from Nephite rule into the land northward. Teancum's force knew precisely where Morianton was headed.

The best confirmation of the sizable scale of the borders by the east sea comes from Helaman 4. Lamanite armies drove the Nephites "into the land Bountiful," but after a time the Nephites counterattacked and regained "even the half of all their [traditional] possessions" (Helaman 4:6, 10, 16). The prophet-brothers Nephi$_2$ and Lehi$_2$ then proceeded to work through the reconquered territory from the north, preaching repentance as they went. Beginning at the city Bountiful, the pair went through Gid, Mulek, and "from one city to another, until they had gone forth among all the people of Nephi who were in the land southward" (see Helaman 5:14–16). That is, when taken together with the land of Bountiful, the lands possessed by the Nephites in what they called the borders by the east sea actually constituted half of their original land-southward possessions. Clearly, the lowlands toward the east sea were a large stretch of real estate. The theater for all this action could not have been a strip of land only, say, five or ten miles in width; it had to have been thirty or forty miles across to make these statements credible.

The nature of the area between the coastal "borders by the east sea" and the mountainous "narrow strip of wilderness" is unclear in the Book of Mormon text, but it involves an important question: Why were the Nephites not concerned about the Lamanites' attacking their homeland by coming out of the wilderness to the south of the lands of Jershon and Moroni and to the east of Manti? Alma 43:22–24 lays out the question. Lamanite armies under one Zerahemnah intended to attack the people of Ammon, who then lived in the land of Jershon, but they were foiled by the armor with which Moroni$_1$ outfitted the Nephite defenders. Not daring to face such odds, they "departed out of the land of Antionum," their base near the east sea, "into the [east] wilderness, and took their journey round about in the wilderness, away by the head of the river Sidon, that they might come into the land of Manti and take possession of the land" (Alma 43:22). Spies followed them for a distance and reported to Moroni$_1$ where they seemed to be headed. The Lamanites' trek to the new target "round about in the wilderness" (Alma 43:24) took them a long time, for Moroni$_1$ had time to send messengers to the prophet Alma$_2$ in Zarahemla to ask him for a revelation on the precise enemy objective, receive the response, then march an army from the east lowlands through the land of Zarahemla to the Manti area, where he laid a trap (see Alma 43:23–25). The likely relationships are displayed on map 5.

MAP 5. LAMANITES GO "ROUND ABOUT"

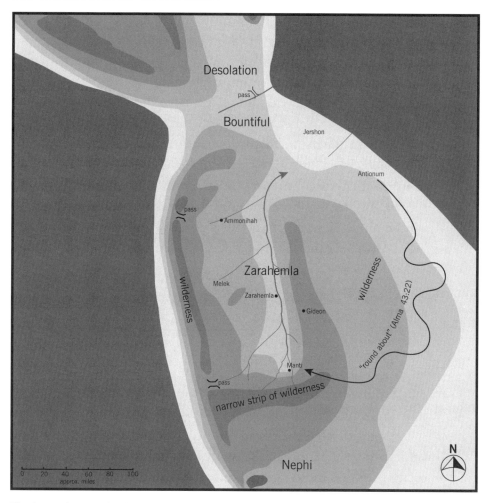

The Lamanite army's trip from the land of Antionum to Manti took long enough for Moroni$_1$ to position his own force in time to intercept them.

On the basis of information about the distances involved in these maneuvers, we can say that the Lamanite march "round about in the wilderness" took weeks. They were in no hurry; they assumed the Nephites would not know where they were headed anyway (see Alma 43:22). But could they not have found a shorter way to get at the Nephite homeland? Why couldn't they have moved from Antionum straight to Gideon and then gone down to Zarahemla in much shorter order? The only reason apparent is that "the wilderness" they were traversing, or skirting, was effectively impassable. Any route they took had to go over a major elevation to get from the eastern lowlands to either Zarahemla or Manti (see Alma 43:25). That barrier had to be the mountainous zone forming the easterly side of the Sidon basin. Judging by travel time, the one way through or around that eastern stretch of wilderness was wide as well as rugged. A statement from Helaman$_2$ to Moroni$_1$ understandably emphasizes that the Lamanites saw no viable targets between Manti and the east sea borders (see Alma 56:25; see also 43:25–26; 59:5–6).

This geographical situation explains why the Lamanite aggressors never made any attempt to penetrate that intimidating wilderness southeast of Zarahemla in order to mount an attack on the capital. For an army, it must have been too tough an ecological nut to crack. The Nephite heartland could count on a natural barrier to shield them from any serious threat from that direction. Combined with the natural mountain barriers that protected their land on their south and west, this wilderness zone in the southeasterly direction helped confer on the Nephites in the center a feeling of complacency about their safety (see Helaman 1:18; Alma 60:19).

What was the course of the Sidon River?

There is convincing reason to suppose that the Sidon reached the sea on the east side of the land southward. It was at least two hundred miles long and located in a tropical environment; thus surely it had a substantial flow. We would expect such a sizable stream to have developed something of a delta where it reached the sea. A delta would explain how such a wide stretch of lowland came into being on the borders by the east sea. When Moroni$_1$ drove Lamanite inhabitants out of the area along the east sea and established garrison cities (see Alma 50:7, 9–11), he focused on fortifying along a defense "line" (Alma 50:11) against anticipated Lamanite attacks. That line logically had a physical basis; it could well have been one of the branch distribution channels by which the waters of the Sidon reached the sea. No comparable piece of coastal land is indicated on the west coast. Quite surely the Sidon did not flow to the west sea, because to the west, we have seen, a mountain range ran—the one that protected the land of Melek. This means that the continental divide was also on the west side. The divide separated streams—likely quite steep and small—that drained into the sea west, the Pacific Ocean, from tributaries of the Sidon River that flowed eastward into the Atlantic.

What can be said about the surface structure of the land northward?

The Nephite record offers limited information about the land northward. The Jaredite record might potentially tell us more, but because we are not clear on all the ways to connect the Nephite and Jaredite maps, we can make only limited use of the geographical information in the book of Ether.

Important geographical facts that Mormon knew about the land northward fail to come through clearly in his record for what seems to me three reasons: (1) While Mormon produced the Book of Mormon in the land northward (see Mormon 6:6), his last few years were highly stressful, so he paid minimal attention to geography. That information would not make any difference to his final message. (2) He may have had a limited supply of unused metal plates and may thus have been reluctant to discuss such details. (3) He was a native of the area where he then lived (see Mormon 1:1–6), and natives of an area are inclined to feel it unnecessary to explain what is obvious to them about that area.

The land northward as characterized in the book of Ether was consistently divided into two politically rivalrous parts. If we had a more detailed text, we might be able to make sure that the division was geographically based, but still that notion makes sense. One part under certain rulers was considered "up"—in elevated terrain—while a rival occupied another portion in lowlands.

The land of Moron (no city is ever mentioned) was the Jaredite capital area, "the land of their first inheritance" (Ether 7:16), "where the king dwelt" (Ether 7:5–6). From some Jaredite lands one went "up" to Moron (Ether 7:5; 14:11); at other times coming to or from Moron required travel "over" some elevated feature (see Ether 7:4–5; 9:3, 9).

At times the realm described in Ether's record was divided in two. For example, Ether 7:16–20 reports, "The country was divided; and there were two kingdoms." Jared rebelled against his father, King Omer, and "came and dwelt in the land of Heth" (Ether 8:2), where he gained control of half the kingdom and made his father captive (see Ether 8:3). Restored to rule by loyal sons, Omer was later forced to flee from Moron to the east seashore (see Ether 9:3, discussed below). Ether 10:20; 14:3, 6–7, 11–12, 26; 15:8–11 relate in a complicated way to further show the contrast between upland and lowland. The elevation difference coupled with the division of the land into political halves suggests a continuing environmental and geographical basis for rivalry, probably highlands versus lowlands. The references given show that the lowlands were on the east sea side, while the higher elevation was toward the west sea.

There was, however, a hilly area within the east lowlands near the east sea. Omer's journey took "many days" (Ether 9:3), which suggests a route that was indirect, since Moron was also "near" the land Desolation (Ether 7:6). We are further told that in the course of his trip he "passed by the hill of Shim" and then "came over by the place where the Nephites were destroyed," that is, Cumorah (Ether 9:3). Mormon explained that the retreating Nephites arrived at the hill Shim before they got to Cumorah, indicating that Shim is on the south of Cumorah (see Mormon 4:20–23; compare 6:2–4). Map 6 displays how this information in the text fits together into a consistent picture in relation to the topography.

An obvious physical principle supports the concept that higher lands lay to the west. Notable bodies of water were found in parts of the lowland area not far from the east sea. The waters of Ripliancum, a name meaning "large" or "to exceed all," barred the way northward for the army of Coriantumr$_1$ in the closing days of the Jaredites' final wars (see Ether 15:7–10). From there the hill Ramah, the same place the Nephites called Cumorah (see Ether 9:3; 15:11), was only one day away southward (see Ether 15:10–11). Mormon's description of the Cumorah/Ramah area told of "many waters, rivers, and fountains" (Mormon 6:4). Where did all this water come from? Clearly, much of it had to be runoff from highlands that were,

MAP 6. SOME JAREDITE LOCATIONS

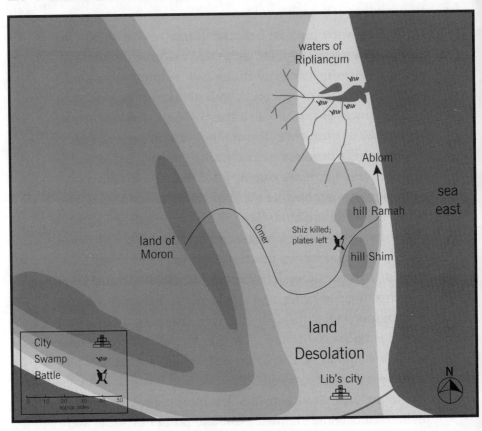

A few Jaredite locations can be related to the Nephite map. For example, from Moron, King Omer "came over," passed by the hill Shim, and then again "came over" past the "place where the Nephites were destroyed" to reach Ablom by the sea (Ether 9:3).

logically, to the west. That westward area included the land of Moron. We have already seen that the high mountains forming the continental divide in the land southward lay near that land's west coast, and it makes geological sense that in the land north from the isthmus the higher areas would also be toward the west.

Two bits of information from the Nephite record confirm the picture of the western part of the land northward being elevated. First, consider the geographical situation within the narrow neck of land. According to the text, only one route allowed large groups to travel from south to north through the neck—via the narrow passage, which was near sea level and not far from the east sea (see Alma 50:25, 29, 31–34; 51:25–26, 30, 32; 52:9). Yet the neck was wide enough for Limhi's explorers to pass through without detecting the presence of either sea. Why could groups not pass into the land northward at a point farther west than the narrow passage? It could well have been because the western side of the isthmus was bounded on the north by a mountain barrier, the southern rampart of the highlands that contained the land of Moron.

The presence of western highlands in the land northward is also confirmed by Hagoth's shipping activity. The settlers who migrated from the land of Zarahemla to the eastern part of the land northward simply "went forth unto the land northward" (Helaman 3:3) "and even . . . did spread forth" (Helaman 3:5; see 3:8). This progressive overland migration, or continuous "spread," no doubt traversed the narrow pass; movements mentioned in Alma 63:4 and 9 also appear to have been overland. Nothing is said nor hinted of the use of shipping along the east sea coast, but we are pointedly informed that along the west sea side, Hagoth and others built ships to move colonists northward (see Alma 63:5–8, 10; Helaman 3:10). Why the difference? It is reasonable to suppose that the west highlands of the land northward extended to the sea and that thus no suitable land route northward existed along the west coast. Furthermore, a highland zone in the western land northward likely meant that few desirable sites for settlement existed along that coast, for the elevated zone would have kept the moist northeast trade winds of the tropics from reaching the west coast. The lack of timber indicated in the Hagoth account (see Helaman 3:10) further indicates that the west coast colonies in the land northward were only marginally viable. If the western highland zone stretched to near the west sea so that no feasible coastal land route existed, this could explain the use of ships.

In any case, those colonies had little long-term impact on Nephite consciousness: the people in the south did not even know what happened to the ships; Alma's son Corianton traveled there only to drop out of sight historically; and none of the west coast colonies are indicated to have been involved in the final wars of the Nephites, all of which took place in the eastern lowlands (see Alma 63:8, 10, 11; Mormon 2:16–6:6).

A unique feature of the land northward is the hilly area (no "mountain" is identified there) near the east sea. It included the hills Cumorah and Shim of the Nephites, and what the Jaredites called hill Comnor and adjacent valleys of Corihor and Shurr (see Mormon 6:4, 11; Ether 9:3; 14:28).

Unfortunately, the information Moroni$_2$ gives us in his abridgement of Ether's account (see Ether 1:1–5), where we might hope to learn about land northward topography, is too brief to allow us to establish more than a partial connection with Nephite geography. Moroni$_2$ specifically identified the hill Ramah with his hill Cumorah (see Ether 9:3; 15:11). Also, the narrow neck of land and by implication the narrow pass were features of the Jaredite lowland sector that Moroni$_2$ tied to Nephite geography (see Ether 9:32–33; 10:20).

Moroni$_2$ also said that the land of Moron was "near" (Ether 7:6) the land of Desolation that he and his father knew well. However, the term "near" is somewhat puzzling, since, as noted earlier, Jaredite king Omer's journey from Moron past Cumorah and to the east seashore was said to take "many days" (Ether 9:3). (The route he followed must have been circuitous.) In any case, nothing Mormon or Moroni₂ said in their own records suggests that Nephites they knew of or cared about settled in or had anything to do with the Moron of the Jaredites in the higlands.

Jaredite territory in the land northward was not very extensive. The story of the end of Ether's ministry underlines that fact. In the days of King Coriantumr, who reigned "over all the land" (Ether 12:1), Ether's prophesying was rejected, and the prophet had to flee from Moron to a "cavity of a rock" (Ether 13:13–14, 18). That rude shelter served as his base while he made the remainder of his record. He got his information on the final wars of his people by "viewing the destructions which came upon the people, by night" (Ether 13:14); somehow he "did behold all the doings of the people" (Ether 15:13). Perhaps this wording means that he had informants, for he himself could not have visited all the battlefields on an overnight basis. He might have been shown visions. (How else could he have learned the details of the final struggle between Shiz and Coriantumr₁, as told in Ether 15:29–32? The only other option would be that Coriantumr₁ himself related that story to the Mulekites [see Omni 1:21], whose record of what Coriantumr₁ told them came to Moroni₂'s attention by the time Moroni₂ was working on the book of Ether.) Finally the Lord told Ether to "go forth," and Ether saw that the destruction he had prophesied had indeed come to pass (see Ether 15:33).

Thus we are left with a broad outline and some particular intimations about the topography and waterways of the land northward, but we cannot solve more than a portion of that puzzle.

Summary

The land surfaces and bodies of water in the Nephites' land of promise as pictured in Mormon's text come through with high consistency. The overall treatment makes complete sense in terms of the principles of geography and the natural sciences. The proposition that Mormon had a clear-cut map in his mind as he produced the Book of Mormon is strongly supported, even though it is frustrating that certain clarifying details are omitted.

The southerly portion of the land southward, the overall land of Nephi, was predominantly highland country, although the term "land of Nephi" in a political sense came to be extended to include limited territories along both the east sea and west sea coasts. Northward from Nephi was a marked mountain barrier that had to be crossed to reach the land of Zarahemla. The basic landform of the land of Zarahemla was a sizable basin drained by the Sidon River, the only river specifically named or characterized in the Book of Mormon. The Nephite lands and cities, including the heartland around the city of Zarahemla, was at an intermediate elevation. The area was closed in by a high range of mountains near the west sea coast and another sizable elevated territory on the east sea side of the basin. A deep zone of "wilderness" sloped down from that eastern upland to extensive coastal lowlands by the east sea, but the west coastal zone was narrow, and the Nephites inhabited it only lightly if at all.

The isthmus, or "narrow neck of land," that connected the lands southward and northward contained a particular feature termed a "narrow pass." Through it all large-scale movements of people through the neck had to travel, making it of absolute strategic importance in warfare. In the land northward, a western upland sector was contrasted with easterly wet lowlands. A knot of hill country near the east sea lay a short distance north of the neck. The crucial position of this pass can be seen very clearly in the case of Morianton's flight (see map 4).

The main topographic features of the Book of Mormon lands in America where the historical events it records took place can be seen on the map entitled Major Physical Features, located on the inside back cover of the book.

Distances and Directions

Theories of how Nephite lands relate to an actual map of the western hemisphere have varied vastly in scale. Where one person has separated a certain city from another by a thousand miles, another may assign only ten. The scale of the lands obviously makes a difference in how we read the Book of Mormon account. What did Mormon believe the distances were as he authored the history? Did he make enough statements on this subject to allow us to establish an intelligent picture of how big or how little the lands of Zarahemla or Nephi were?

Mormon furnished us with a number of key pieces of information from which we can establish distances:

1. The journeys of Alma$_1$'s people (Mosiah 18:1–7, 31–34; 23:1–3, 25–26; 24:18–25)
2. Limhi's explorers' expedition to the land northward (Mosiah 8:7–9; 21:25–27)
3. Movements in the Amlicite war (Alma 2)
4. Alma$_2$'s circuit of cities preaching repentance (Alma 5–15)
5. The wars in the borders by the east sea and in the southwest quarter (Alma 43–62:42)

6. The land of Nephi as described in the Zeniffite account and that of the sons of Mosiah₂ (Mosiah 7–22; Alma 17–26)
7. The last wars between Nephites and Lamanites (Mormon 2–6)

What can we learn about distances from the story of Alma₁ and his people?

A party of a few hundred people under the leadership of Alma₁ assembled in a place called Mormon, which was "in the borders of the land" of Nephi (Mosiah 18:4). On the basis of Mosiah 18:31–34, we can infer that Mormon lay a distance of from one to three days' normal travel (from fifteen to forty miles by foot) from the city of Nephi.[26] To escape pursuers sent by King Noah, the group fled at top speed (but with women and children and animal herds necessarily holding them back) eight days' travel into the wilderness through the uplands northward from Nephi to the land they called Helam (see Mosiah 23:1–4, 19). After a few years there they had to escape again; this time it took them thirteen days to reach the land of Zarahemla (see Mosiah 24:20–25).[27] Adding these distances together, we arrive at a total of about twenty-two or twenty-three days' foot travel between the city of Nephi and the city of Zarahemla. A portion of the route taken by Alma's people is shown on map 11.

From an extensive body of accounts of ancient and modern travel under conditions like those prevailing for Alma's people, we can be fairly confident that they traveled at a rate of about 11 miles per day, give or take a little.[28] The distance they covered on the ground would have been 250 miles in round numbers, including twists and turns through mountainous country. The beeline distance between the two cities would more likely be on the order of 180 miles. Roughly half that should have taken the party to the middle of the narrow strip of wilderness—the watershed—that separated the highlands of Nephi from the drainage of the Sidon River. The actual territory inhabited by the Nephites would probably have extended no more than 75 miles upstream from the city of Zarahemla to the local land of Manti, the southernmost settled point within the greater land of Zarahemla (see Alma 58:14).

Having established this southern dimension, we can extend our map northward from Zarahemla on the basis of Moroni$_1$'s letter to the chief judge, Pahoran$_1$. Moroni$_1$ referred to the city of Zarahemla as being in the "heart" of the land of the Nephites (Alma 60:19, 22). That position is generally confirmed by dissenter Coriantumr$_2$'s daring invasion that came out of Nephi to capture the city of Zarahemla, in the "center" of the land of Zarahemla (see Helaman 1:17–18, 24–27). However, "center" may have been more conceptual than entirely literal. Coriantumr$_2$ burst upon the city's defenders with almost no warning, which suggests a relatively short distance from the frontier to the capital city of Zarahemla. But the invaders soon found themselves bogged down farther downstream in what was called "the most capital parts of the land" (Helaman 1:27). This terminology suggests that a stretch of additional cities and heavy population lay northerly from the city of Zarahemla for a somewhat greater distance than on the upper stretch of the river. If the upper river was 75 miles long, the stretch downstream from the city of Zarahemla might have been, say, 100 miles northward.

Northward beyond the land of Zarahemla proper (at least as the boundaries were construed at one point in time) lay an unlabeled, no doubt small, land "between the land Zarahemla and the land Bountiful" (3 Nephi 3:23). It is referred to only once. If this unnamed land and the land Bountiful were each 30 miles from north to south, then the straight-line distance from the city of Zarahemla to the boundary between Bountiful and the land Desolation—the northern limit of the land southward—adds up to a total of 160 miles. That means that from the city of Nephi to where the land northward began was roughly 340 miles on a direct line.

These are estimates, of course, yet they are not likely to be a long way off, because they are based on how fast actual groups have been able to travel in a day. Given the uncertainties that we cannot avoid when interpreting the statements in the record, it would be no shock to find someday that the numbers are off by 25 percent, but it is difficult for me to believe that they could be as much as 50 percent in error. In other words, on Mormon's mental map, the land southward stretched only a few hundred miles in length. (Keep in mind that Palestine from Dan to Beersheba was only about 150 miles long.)

How about the distance into the land northward? Crucial information comes from the account of the exploring party Zeniffite king Limhi sent to locate Zarahemla. Their purpose was to request help from the Nephites to free Limhi's people from Lamanite bondage. The expedition consisted of forty-three of his most "diligent" men (see Mosiah 8:7–8). It had been two generations since their fathers had come from Zarahemla, and tradition apparently did not furnish firm information about the route they should follow to reach Zarahemla. The explorers wandered for many days before discovering extensive ruins. These ruins turned out to be in the land Desolation of the Jaredites, for there the party came upon corroded artifacts and the gold plates on which the last Jaredite prophet, Ether, had written his account of that peoples' history and extermination (see Ether 15:33). The explorers then backtracked to the city of Nephi, their homeland, bearing Ether's record and a few Jaredite relics as proof of their story. What is remarkable to us now is their conclusion that the remains they found had been left by the inhabitants of Zarahemla, who they supposed must somehow have been destroyed (see Mosiah 21:26). We now understand that the exploring party had traveled all the way into the land northward, to within a few miles of the hill Ramah/Cumorah. Map 7 shows a plausible route for their expedition.

How far had they traveled in miles? What distance can we infer it was from the city of Nephi to the place where Ether left the plates, which was near the hill Ramah/Cumorah? Surely they would have known from their grandfathers' traditions approximately how far it was to Zarahemla, so if we put ourselves in their sandals, we probably would have begun to wonder, after the estimated number of days had passed, just how much farther northward to press on. When they found no inhabited Zarahemla or, apparently, any people with whom they could talk, they must have begun to think about turning back. I can imagine them going on for perhaps twice as many days as the tradition told them it would take to get to Zarahemla, but not a lot more. We know that Nephi was separated from Zarahemla by less than two hundred miles, so it seems improbable that those diligent men would have pressed northward much more than double that distance without arguing among themselves about turning back. It looks from this incident like the final Jaredite battlefield was not much more than four hundred airline miles from Nephi. Again, these are estimates and could be off by some, but not by a major amount.

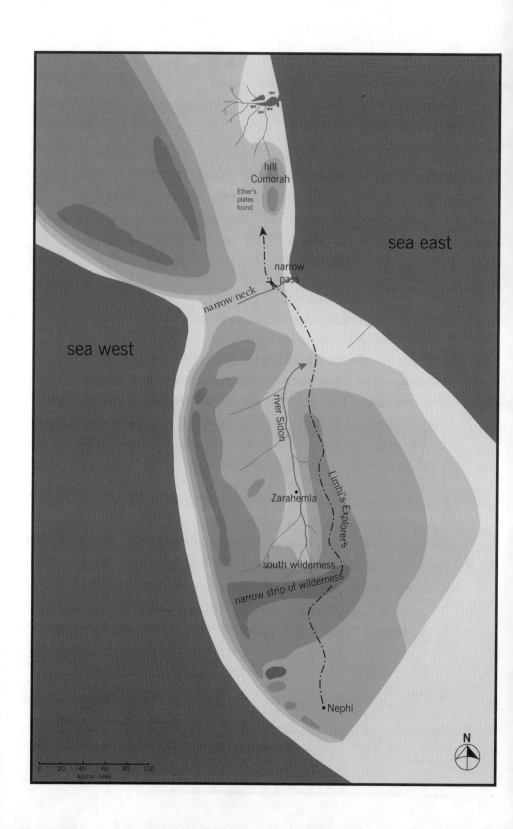

How big was the immediate territory around Zarahemla?

Consider an incident that involved territory on a much smaller scale than the distance traveled by Limhi's searchers. Alma 2:15–37; 3:2; and 4:2 inform us about the scene of a pair of battles in the immediate vicinity of Zarahemla. A people called the Amlicites, dissenters from the Nephite government who probably came from farther down the Sidon River,[29] gathered at the hill Amnihu, just across the river from the city of Zarahemla, to battle against the Nephite army. The loyalists under chief judge Alma$_2$ seemed to get the better of the fight, and the rebels headed up to the valley of Gideon (we have already seen that at that point they would have been on the preferred—and probably fastest—route southward in the direction of Manti). When night stopped the pursuit, the Nephites camped in the valley, but under cover of night and on a convenient road, the Amlicites hightailed it on southward. Alma$_2$'s scouts hurried back at daybreak to report dismaying news: the enemy force had got to the river Sidon, crossed it, and joined forces with a Lamanite army that had timed its invasion (surely by secret advance planning with the rebel leader Amlici) to be at that point that morning. Now the combined enemy groups were swarming down the west bank of the river toward the city of Zarahemla. This word set off a race between Alma$_2$'s army and the enemy to determine who could reach the city first. Alma$_2$ aimed straight for a crucial point, a ford across the river just upstream from the city, and started to cross just as the Lamanites showed up. In a desperate fight, the Nephites

MAP 7. LIMHI'S EXPLORERS
A wrong turn in the wilderness no doubt got this expedition on a wrong track, perhaps as shown. Returning home, they would have followed familiar landmarks back along the same route.

sent their opponents fleeing toward a nearby forest "wilderness" (Alma 2:37) called Hermounts. Within hours, the escaping force was scattered and the Nephites arrived at the city they had just saved. Map 8 represents the positions where these events took place and the distances separating them.

The entire episode consumed two days and one night. The distances cannot be much different than this: hill Amnihu to Gideon, no more than twenty miles; Gideon direct to the ford at the river, maybe twelve miles; Zarahemla to Minon, not over thirty-five miles; Zarahemla city to the river ford, less than ten miles; the battle scene at the river bank to the wilderness of Hermounts, not much greater than ten miles. When we analyze the detailed narrative of this thirty-six-hour period, the realities imposed by travel conditions simply do not allow much leeway in these numbers.

What dimensions are revealed by Alma₂'s missionary journey around the land?

Alma$_2$ set out to establish the church in areas toward the limits of the land of Zarahemla as it existed in his day. He began at Gideon, then headed to Melek, Ammonihah, and Sidom. At one point in time he also started to go to the city of Aaron but did not reach it. Finally, he returned from Sidom to his home in Zarahemla. The account yields distance figures that are not precise but are still useful (see Alma 8:3–6, 13; 15:18). To Melek from Zarahemla required significant travel: Alma$_1$ departed from Zarahemla "and took his journey over into the land of Melek, on the west of the river Sidon, on the west by

---

MAP 8. THE AMLICITE CONFLICT
All these movements took place within a thirty-six-hour period. That means that the scale of the action covered only tens of miles.

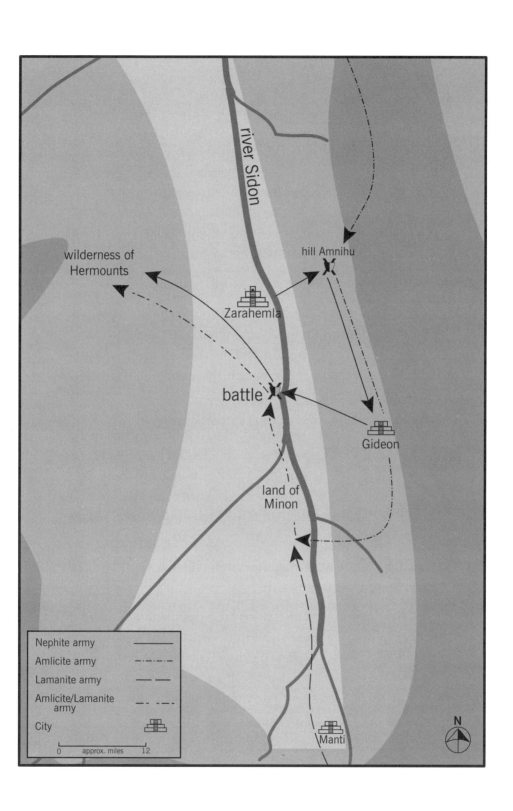

river Sidon

wilderness of
Hermounts

hill Amnihu

Zarahemla

battle

Gideon

land of
Minon

Nephite army

Amlicite army

Lamanite army

Amlicite/Lamanite
army

City

0   approx. miles   12

Manti

N

the borders of the wilderness" (Alma 8:3). This sounds rather more complicated than when he "went over upon the east of the river Sidon, into the valley of Gideon" (Alma 6:7). The Gideon trip would have taken him only one day, we have just seen from the Amlicite affair. "Took his journey over into" Melek implies greater distance. (At the end of his life, Alma$_2$'s last trip followed the same course; "he departed out of the land of Zarahemla, as if to go into the land of Melek" [Alma 45:18], but he was never seen again. The implication of this passage confirms that the journey was not a short, simple one.) Two or three days of travel seem called for to reach Melek, perhaps fifty miles or more. From Melek it then took Alma$_2$ three days' travel northward to reach Ammonihah (see Alma 8:6), say another fifty-plus miles.[30] Traveling from Ammonihah to Sidom (the name suggests that it was at the Sidon River) should have taken roughly the same time and distance as a journey from Zarahemla to Melek (see Alma 15:1). And finally from Sidom to Zarahemla, back up the river, would again have roughly reversed the distance from Melek to Ammonihah—three days' travel. All these numbers are sensible when compared with the earlier discussion of Zarahemla as being in the "center" of the land of Zarahemla. (See map 9.)

How far did the Nephite possessions stretch along the east coast in the land southward?

Details about the marches by the Nephite and Lamanite armies in the area called the borders by the east seashore can also be converted into plausible distances. We begin with Alma 52:18–31. Moroni$_1$, Lehi$_2$, and Teancum and the military units they commanded began to decoy a Lamanite army out of the fortified city of Mulek by sending a small group near the city. The Lamanites pursued them in full force, thinking they could

MAP 9. ALMA$_2$'S PREACHING CIRCUIT

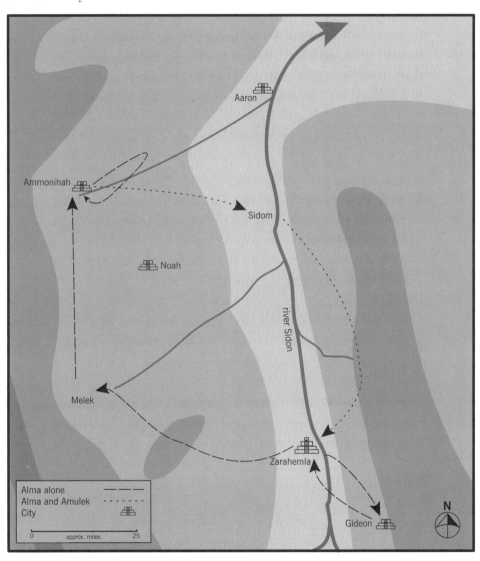

In his travels, Alma$_2$ established the church "throughout all the land" (Alma 16:21), so he must have essentially circled the territory in the Sidon River basin that contained most of the Nephite population.

easily capture them. The decoy party retreated toward the city Bountiful "down by the seashore, northward" (Alma 52:23), leading the Lamanites away "until they came near the city Bountiful" (Alma 52:27). A new Nephite force from Bountiful then appeared, causing the Lamanites to stop and turn about, worried lest they not be able to reach their city because they "were wearied because of their long march" (Alma 52:28, 31; Alma 51:33 indicates that "the heat of the day" was debilitating). Part of Moroni$_1$'s unit had by this time overcome the tiny garrison left to guard the stronghold, Mulek, while the rest of his men hurried to confront the Lamanites. Caught between armies, the Lamanites were all slain or captured (see Alma 52:38–39), and the prisoners were marched to Bountiful.

The day's action saw the Lamanites move from Mulek to near Bountiful (say two-thirds of the distance) and then retreat part of the way back to Mulek. Their weariness probably meant that their total travel was more than a torrid day's travel under battle conditions, say about eighteen miles along an irregular trail. On a beeline, Bountiful to Mulek might then be on the order of twelve miles.

From Mulek to Gid should be roughly the same distance (perhaps a normal day's walking for a merchant). However, when we compare Helaman 5:14–15 with Alma 51:26, we learn that one could as readily go from Bountiful to Gid as from Bountiful to Mulek. Consequently, Gid was directly inland from Mulek and thus no farther southward in relation to the seashore.[31] The next city to the south that the Lamanites had captured was Omner. Insufficient data are given to figure an actual distance from Omner to Gid or Mulek, but it is reasonable that it was of about the same order, in this case let us say twenty miles. This would put Omner thirty miles southward from Bountiful, measuring along the shore.

In the next operation, Moroni$_1$'s army captured the city of Nephihah (see Alma 62:26), which was inland some distance from the shore (see Alma 50:14–15; compare 59:5–8). From there they immediately marched to attack the city of Lehi (see Alma 62:30). The dislodged Lamanites fled northward "from city to city" (Alma 62:32), probably including Morianton and Omner. Before they had fled far they were met by a Nephite army advancing southward from Gid and Mulek. The Lamanites had nowhere to go except to scramble along near the beach ("even down upon the borders by the seashore" [Alma 62:32]) until just before dark they reached the city of Moroni, the last city still held by the Lamanites (see Alma 62:33–35).

The text indicates that capture of Nephihah, the flight from Lehi "from city to city" northward, then turning back all the way to Moroni was a single military operation done in a single day. How far was it in miles? With their lives on the line, the Lamanites might have made twenty-five or more miles total (Alma 62:35 says that by dark, both the Lamanites and Nephites "were weary because of the greatness of the march"). Some of those twenty-five miles were seaward and some were consumed by the futile doubling back to and from the north. The total distance the Lamanites traveled southward parallel to the beach could hardly have been more than fifteen miles.

In summary, the mileages measured along the coast are as follows: Bountiful to Gid/Mulek, twelve miles; Gid/Mulek to Omner, twenty miles; the southward component of the last day's flight, maximum fifteen miles. Suppose we now arbitrarily allow an additional twenty miles for the distance between Omner and Lehi, for which we do not have a specific basis for measurement, another ten miles from Bountiful to the "line" that separated the lands Bountiful and Desolation, and finally, five miles from Moroni city to the edge ("line") of

Nephite-controlled land. Adding the numbers together we conclude that the southward limit of Nephite possessions along the east sea was only about eighty miles from the land northward. No wonder Amalickiah, in his plan to capture the narrow neck (see Alma 51:30), chose this east shore as his prime point of attack (the distance he would have had to drive along the west coast was over 250 miles). Further, no wonder Moroni$_1$ put such prodigious effort into fortifying the Nephites' vulnerable east coast (see Alma 50:7–11).

How wide was the land southward?

The Book of Mormon relates four local lands and their cities that spread across the land southward from east to west: Moroni, Nephihah, Aaron, and Ammonihah. The land of Moroni, a small territory near the east seashore and close to the Lamanite possessions, bordered on the land of Nephihah, which was also, broadly speaking, in the borders by the east sea (see Alma 50:13–14). The territory administered by Nephihah also abutted on the land of Aaron (see Alma 50:14).

The position of Aaron has posed a problem for some students of Nephite geography; Aaron, which on the one hand ties to Nephihah, which was near the southerly limit of Nephite holdings on the east coast, on the other hand relates to Ammonihah, which was near the west wilderness in the northerly section of the land of Zarahemla (see Alma 8:13; 16:2).[32] Once we realize, however, how short the stretch of Nephite-controlled east sea coast was, the conflict that some have seen between the statements about Aaron's position is resolved. The center of the land around the city of Aaron was apparently lightly settled (no other city is ever named in that sector), so it is probable that Aaron administered a rather large area, which reached so far toward the east (probably down the Sidon River) that its limit on the east reached the westernmost territory under Nephihah's control. When the positions of the four lands—Moroni, Nephihah, Aaron, and Ammonihah—are plotted on a map (see map 10) that allows us to compare the spread among them with other distances, the total width from coast to coast across the land southward comes out to be on the order of two hundred miles.

Only two textual passages relate directly to the question of the width of the land southward. Both bits of information are in reference to the area near the narrow neck. First, Mormon's summary geography in Alma 22:32 states, "Now, it was only

MAP 10. SPATIAL RELATIONS OF FOUR CITIES ACROSS THE LAND SOUTHWARD

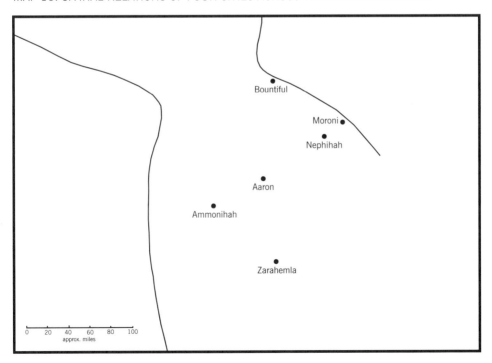

The geographical relationships among the four lands that stretch across the land southward are clarified when the comparative distances separating them are carefully inferred.

the distance of a day and a half's journey for a Nephite, on the line Bountiful and the land Desolation, from the east to the west sea . . . there being a small neck of land between the land northward and the land southward." The other scripture, Helaman 4:5–7, tells of Nephite armies that were driven northward by Lamanites around 30 B.C. The Nephites were expelled completely from the land of Zarahemla and from their territory along the west coast, ultimately stopping at the south edge of the land of Bountiful (see Helaman 4:6). The Nephites no doubt retreated along the same route out of Zarahemla, via the pass near Ammonihah and the west coast, as did the Nephites under Mormon over three centuries later (see Mormon 2:5–7). At the south boundary of the land Bountiful at the west sea, they fortified a line that stretched "from the west sea, even unto the east; it being a day's journey for a Nephite, [on] the line which they had fortified and stationed their armies to defend their north country" (Helaman 4:7). This fortified line did not extend across the narrow neck of land; its purpose was only to block the west coastal plain. Thus the "day's journey," whatever it measured, had nothing to do with the width across the entire neck, for that did not begin until farther northward, on the other side of Bountiful. (See "Mormon's Map" on the inside front cover of the book.)

Alma 22:32 speaks directly about the narrow neck, but the meaning of its statement, a "day and a half's journey for a Nephite," is unclear. Both this phrase and "a day's journey for a Nephite" (Helaman 4:7) are expressions that reach us through Mormon, a military man, and may reflect some standard measure of distance familiar among Nephite military people. Furthermore, several researchers have observed that the phrase in Alma 22:32, "from the east to the west sea," allows the interpretation that the journey was measured some point short of the actual east sea shore.[33] After all, it would be foolish for the Nephites to waste resources defending a line that reached the sea to the east of the narrow pass, since their enemies could not reach the land northward other than via the pass (see Mormon 3:5–6; 4:4, 19).

In any case, the actual distance a person can go in one day varies greatly according to setting, individual capacity, and mode of travel. Persons have been known to travel over one hundred miles per day by foot with some regularity, and of course if one went down a river in a canoe, an even greater distance could be traveled.[34] Such variables prevent us from establishing a definite length for the "line" at the neck, but a range of figures between 60 and 125 miles can be argued as reasonable for the "day and a half's journey." (Recall that the narrower one makes the neck, the more difficult it is to explain how Limhi's explorers failed to realize that they had passed through it.)

What can we learn about distances in the land of Nephi from the story of the Zeniffites and the travels of the sons of Mosiah₂?

Events in the reigns of the Zeniffite kings Noah and Limhi shed light on distances in the local land of Nephi and its vicinity (the land and city at that time were called Lehi-Nephi, probably at the insistence of the Lamanite overlords, but for simplicity we will use the old term, Nephi). Noah "built a tower near the temple [in the city of Nephi], even so high that he could stand upon the top thereof and overlook the land of Shilom, and also the land of Shemlon, which was possessed by the Lamanites" (Mosiah 11:12). From this tower Noah spotted a Lamanite army coming up out of the land of Shemlon toward Nephi (see Mosiah 19:6). For a Zeniffite to have such a view, the distance to Shilom could hardly have exceeded ten miles and the near border of Shemlon would have been within twenty miles. Moreover, Lamanite armies consistently came "up" from Shemlon to Shilom and Nephi, and even farther "up" to hilly land overlooking those two places (see Mosiah 7:5–6; 10:8; 20:7–9). Shilom and Shemlon seem to have been located in the same broad valley as the city and local land of Nephi.

We saw above how the information on the movements of Alma$_1$'s people after they fled from Noah's Zeniffites is important in establishing distances in the Nephi highlands. We can add to that that the land of Amulon was not far from Nephi. The Lamanite army pursued the fleeing people of Limhi but lost their track after two days (under fifty miles). After wandering about trying to find their way back to Nephi, those Lamanites stumbled onto the land of Amulon (see Mosiah 22:16; 23:30–31, 35). Still confused about how to reach Nephi, after leaving Amulon they came across the land of Helam, still lost, yet both lands were no more than eighty-five miles direct from Nephi. The implication is strong from this affair that the terrain was very broken. These relationships are shown on map 11.

That the land of Nephi and its vicinity were small in dimensions is confirmed by the account of Nephi$_1$'s initial settling of it. When Nephi$_1$ and his group left the land of first inheritance on the shore of the west sea, they were penetrating raw wilderness as far as they were concerned. It was probably forested, since they were in the tropics at or near sea level, and they are not said to have had any special divine guidance about routes to take or avoid. The fact that they traveled "many days" (2 Nephi 5:7) thus need not mean a great distance (in 1 Nephi 17:4, 20–21, "many years" turns out to be only eight). They ended up in what was thereafter called the land of Nephi (see

MAP 11. THE FLIGHT OF ALMA₁'S AND LIMHI'S PEOPLES

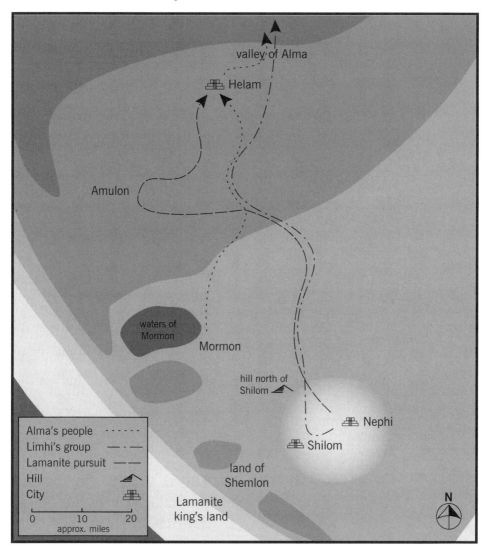

The paths of three groups—Alma₁'s, Limhi's, and a Lamanite army—illustrate the difficulty of finding a way to and from Nephi through mountainous wilderness.

2 Nephi 5:7–8), after traveling possibly eighty to one hundred miles. The distance would have been much shorter on a straight line. Inasmuch as Nephi₁'s people were attacked by the Lamanites within the first generation (see 2 Nephi 5:34), the land of Nephi could not have been far from the coastal land where the Lamanites apparently remained.

Many Lamanites were still living in the west coast wilderness after 100 B.C., yet by then some had moved to higher ground (see Mosiah 24:1–2; Alma 24:20). The Lamanite ruler apparently had only recently moved up to Nephi at the time when Zeniff negotiated with him (see Mosiah 9:5–8); when the exploitable Zeniffites came along, the Lamanites moved out of the decrepit old Nephite city to territory down closer to the lowlands that had been their base in earlier centuries (see Jarom 1:9; Omni 1:2–5; Mosiah 24:2). Eventually, their kings made their permanent capital in upland Nephi (see Alma 22:1).

The travels of the sons of Mosiah₂ as teachers among the Lamanites confirm the small scale of the lands in and around Nephi. For example, the brothers all got together to confer about the problem of protecting their converts (see Alma 24:5), and all the believers lived close enough together that they departed from the land as one body (see Alma 27:14). But the text does not provide information on travel times and mileage in their day.

The account of Aaron₃'s ministry in the city of Jerusalem and the village of Ani-Anti suggests something about the size of "the waters of Mormon." When he separated from his colleagues at the beginning of their work, Aaron₃ first stopped at the city of Jerusalem, which "was away joining the borders of [the waters of] Mormon" (Alma 21:1–2). In Alma₁'s day, Mormon was considered a mere "place" (Mosiah 18:4, 16) that was adjacent to the waters of Mormon, but later the locality

was considered a "land" (Alma 5:3). At the time of the catastrophe when the Savior was crucified, Jerusalem was "sunk"
and waters covered it (see 3 Nephi 9:6–7): it is plausible that
Jerusalem was adjacent to the waters of Mormon and it was
these waters that covered the sunken city. When Aaron₃ left Jerusalem he "came over to a village," yet the land of Mormon is
never mentioned (Alma 21:11). It appears from all this that
Jerusalem and Mormon were miles apart, although they both
adjoined the same body of waters. Consequently, that body
seems to have been a substantial lake a number of miles across.

What can we learn about distances from the final Nephite and Jaredite wars?

Certain information on distances has already been referred
to in chapter 4 on the topography of the land northward where
it was essential for handling that topic.

Mormon spent his early years in the land northward, not
far from where his people would meet extinction more than
half a century later (see 4 Nephi 1:48; Mormon 1:2–6; 2:16–17).
As a youth he moved to the land of Zarahemla, where he soon
was given command over the Nephite army (see Mormon 1:6;
2:1–2). In short order, a Lamanite attack out of the land of Nephi
forced the Nephite army by stages all the way to the city of
Jashon, which was near Mormon's homeland in the land northward (see Mormon 2:3–17). The retreat of a few hundred miles
was across terrain with which Mormon was already familiar.

Back and forth over the same stretch of territory the conflict raged for the next several decades. Once the Nephites even
regained their Zarahemla homeland, but only temporarily (see
Mormon 2:27). At length Mormon ended up near his original
homeland (see Mormon 3:5; 4:1–23). In Mormon's old age the
Nephites retreated farther still, to the city of Jordan and beyond

(see Mormon 5:3, 7). His people being left with few resources, Mormon had to strike a final deal with the Lamanite enemy: to meet them, by appointment, at a mutually acceptable battleground (see Mormon 6:2). Cumorah was the specified site for the climactic struggle. The Lamanites surely must have wanted to get the war over without extending their lines of supply still farther northward, while the Nephites hoped not to lose what territory (including the land of Cumorah) they still controlled. (Further, Cumorah must have been close to, if not actually at, where Mormon had grown up. Perhaps by fighting on territory with which he was intimately familiar, he "had hope to gain [tactical] advantage over the Lamanites" [Mormon 6:4].) The Cumorah rendezvous spot logically would have been on the boundary separating the two parties at that moment.

What all this retreating and advancing means for our consideration of distances is that the Nephites fought out their last decades on familiar ground, none of which was much farther north than the land of Cumorah. We have already established from the story of Limhi's explorers how far that was from the narrow neck. Mormon's personal record thus confirms that the last Nephites never retreated northward much more than one hundred miles north of the narrow pass.

That also means that the lands they possessed were within the same general area where the Jaredites fought their final wars. (As a matter of fact, the successor people in the area, the apostate Nephites, may have considered themselves fated to have the decision about their future decided in the same manner as their predecessors', in battle at the same hill, and perhaps at a related calendrical point—hence the appointed date with the Lamanites. Consider Alma 46:22: "We shall be destroyed, even as *our brethren* in the land northward, if we shall fall into transgression.") The area of the Jaredites' last wars was sufficiently restricted that in some manner it was possible for Ether to go "forth viewing the things which should come upon the people" and complete the remainder of his record (see Ether 13:13–14). The general geographic position of the final Jaredite battles was the eastern portion of the land northward (see Ether 14:12–14, 26; 15:8, 10–11). Moroni$_2$ specifies that some of that area was indeed where the Nephites later operated (see Ether 7:6; 9:3, 31–32; 10:19–21; 15:11, 33). The information we can glean from the record of Ether agrees that the distances involved in the Jaredite wars were similar to those we find in Mormon's record of the Nephites' final decades.

Incidentally, the territories the Nephites colonized via the narrow pass seem to have borne a name of their own in the record: "north countries" or "north country." Mormon and Moroni$_2$ use one of these expressions five times (see Helaman 4:7; Mormon 2:3; Ether 1:1; 9:35; 13:11). Only once does the counterterm "south countries" occur (Mormon 6:15). "North country" and "north countries" seem to me from the contexts to be applied only to the inhabited lowland portions of the land northward that were reached from "the south countries" overland via the narrow pass. But neither "north countries" nor "north country" is used in regard to the colonies along the west sea coast, which are described strictly as being in the "land northward."

Summary on distances

In Mormon's mind, the scene of the Nephite, Lamanite, and Jaredite activities was of limited size. Main lands, minor lands, mountain ranges, plains, valleys, rivers, and oceans are all referred to in a manner that indicates that Mormon not only knew about those geographical elements from the records of his ancestors, but he knew much of the scene personally and intimately. The dimensions are small, although hardly tiny. The promised land in which the Nephites' history played out was on the order of five hundred miles long and over two hundred miles wide, according to Mormon's mental map. That is still considerably larger than the stage on which most Old Testament events took place.

Were Nephite directions the same as those we are familiar with today?

The real question is, what concepts of direction were our primary historian-editor, Mormon, using? We have already seen that he had his own framework for thinking and writing about distances. His ideas of how far apart sites were seem to be consistent even though they are not the same as the scale that governs our thinking in a day of jet travel and worldwide information. "Many days" of travel probably elicited for Mormon a rather different mental image of distance than it would for us. (For that matter, among ourselves the expression brings forth varying ideas.) Similarly, we might ask, would "year" have meant the same to him as it does to us? Lasting how long? Beginning and ending when? Composed of what seasonal variations in climate?

When we examine the text of the Book of Mormon carefully, we can detect numerous places where cultural assumptions that were second nature to the Nephites are quite different than those we hold. We Latter-day Saints may have become so used to "liken[ing] all scriptures unto us" (1 Nephi 19:23) that we assume we understand ideas in them that actually are foreign to our experience. For example, Mosiah 19:20 describes King Noah's being executed "by fire" at the hands of some of his disgusted, angry subjects. Verse 24 goes on, "After they had ended the ceremony, . . . they returned to the land of Nephi."

Not a word in the record sheds light on this or any other ceremony connected with death. To the record keeper, the need for and nature of the ceremony was so obvious that there was no need to explain further. Another instance of unexplained culture is a statement in Mosiah. Alma$_2$, the high priest over "the church" (Mosiah 26:8), put a question of religious policy to King Mosiah$_2$, and the king then "consulted with his priests" on the matter (Mosiah 27:1). Who were these priests? They were not part of the church structure that Alma$_2$ headed, and nowhere else is there an indication that Mosiah$_2$ had his own set of priests. Furthermore, we discover that at other points, Nephite and Lamanite notions, like many Israelite concepts in the Old Testament, varied profoundly from the ideas we hold today. For example, why would a king bow himself in front of his own people and "plead" (Mosiah 20:25) with them for what he desired? What were "dragons" (Alma 43:44)? How did Nephite concepts of "heaven" or "hell" (for example, see Alma 54:11) relate to ones we accept? What did they think the outer zone above the earth (our "space") was like?

There are many points of similarity, of course, between their concepts and ours. Much of the thought and experience conveyed in the ancient records relates sufficiently to the symbols and meanings familiar in our culture that we can learn much from studying them. But differences need to be recognized, not ignored.

Direction is one such concept. The world's varied cultures have produced remarkably diverse models of spatial dimensions on the face of the earth. For example, certain Inuit (Eskimos) who lived north of the Arctic Circle, where the sun is not visible for a good part of the year, used alternative terminology in place of our east, west, north, and south, which were essentially useless to them. They spoke of directions as "above versus below," in reference to local elevations, and spoke of "inside versus outside," an arbitrary contrast that makes sense only in terms of their traditions.[35] In ancient Mesopotamia, the Sumerians based their directions on the prevailing winds, which they considered to blow from what we call northwest, northeast, southeast, and southwest; following that tradition, the later Babylonians oriented their maps so that northwest was at the top.[36] In ancient Mesoamerica, "Maya spatial orientation to the four corners of their universe is not based upon our cardinal directions of N, S, E, W, but probably either upon inter-cardinal points (i.e. NE, NW, SW, SE) or upon two directions in the East and two directions in the West (i.e. sunrise at winter solstice, sunrise at summer solstice [which are 50 degrees apart] sunset at winter solstice and sunset at summer solstice)."[37] Such varied examples are everywhere.[38] To those who share a particular culture, their way of labeling invariably seems "obvious" and does not require explanation, while all other schemes seem to them strange.

One thing we learn from studying this material is that the cardinal directions—east, west, south, north—have not been basic to the directional schemes of most of the world's cultures. What our culture has taught us, that the cardinal directions are obvious, is not true historically.

We may be tempted to think automatically that "northward" and "southward" label directions that are the same as "north" and "south." But "northward" signals a different concept than does "north," something like "in a general northerly direction." By their frequency of using the *–ward* suffix, we can infer that Mormon and his ancestors used a somewhat different cultural scheme for directions than we do.[39] However, we cannot tell from the Book of Mormon text exactly how their concepts differed from ours, because all we have to work with is the English translation provided through Joseph Smith.

The subtlety directional matters can show is displayed in a system of contrasts that most of us may have missed in Mormon's account. These contrasts are in the use of the terms "came" and "went." For example, in the first Lamanite attack on the city of Ammonihah, the text says that the Lamanites had "come in" to the land (Alma 16:2; compare 49:6, "come upon"), but when the same incident was related later, the text says they "went over" (Alma 25:2). Similar differences between "came" and "went" are shown repeatedly. Nobody has yet analyzed this word usage systematically, but a reasonable guess to explain it is that the distinction had to do with the location of the historian at the time he wrote his record. In the case of the attack on Ammonihah, the version of the story that used "come" was part of the Nephite record prepared and kept in Zarahemla, while the second report was from the record of, and thus from the point of view of, the sons of Mosiah$_1$, who at that time were dwelling in the land of Nephi.

These examples suggest that we still have a ways to go before we even know all the right questions about Nephite direction systems that we should ask of the text. At this stage in our study of Mormon's record, we will do well to take advantage of the caution caveat lector, or "let the reader beware." Beware of making assumptions about meanings that may prove to be misleading because they spring from modern-day assumptions rather than from ancient ways. The Book of Mormon text, like all scripture, is subtle; full understanding of it demands extensive and intensive study that uses all the tools at our disposal. Relying on our own ethnocentric interpretations is not an approach to be recommended.

chapter 6

*T*he Environment of the Nephites
and How They Exploited It

My mental map of my own country not only includes features that are an inherent part of nature but also depends on how we have come to transform raw nature through our activities. For me, California means more than sheer physical elements like the Sierra Nevada mountains, the Mojave desert, and the giant forests of the north. It also means citrus and avocado groves in southern California, the vast canals and cultivated fields of the Central Valley, and the urban transformation of the Bay Area. A complete understanding of Book of Mormon geography must likewise involve the ways in which the activities of the Nephites, Lamanites, and Jaredites altered the natural landscape. Mormon's mental map of Nephite and Lamanite territories involved such cultural effects on nature as the clearing of forests to prepare land for planting, the making of roads and trails, and the development of a port where ships were built and launched. For us to understand his sense of geography, we must appreciate how the ancient inhabitants transformed their environment for economic and social ends and the geographical consequences those activities produced.

We cannot attempt a full reconstruction of Nephite economy; that would require a book by itself. All we try to do here is discover some of the important ways in which the economic exploitation of the environment in which the Nephites lived surely colored Mormon's picture of his world.

What was the climate where the Nephites and Lamanites dwelt?

Climatic conditions are crucial to how a people interpret and utilize their land. As a first step toward characterizing the climate in which Book of Mormon groups lived, let us note that the only part of the New World that can qualify as the promised land on the basis of configuration—that is, possessing the somewhat hourglass shape that we saw in chapter 3—is Middle America, that part of the hemisphere south of the United States and north of South America. Based on its shape the promised land settled by Lehi$_1$ and his descendants as recorded in the Book of Mormon has to be somewhere in that area. Nearly all that territory is tropical or semitropical (although parts of the highlands are essentially temperate). It is fair to say, then, that Nephi$_1$'s ship landed in tropical America; consequently, the "land of first inheritance" of the Nephites and Lamanites was rather hot and rainy and had lots of vegetation. (Such a climate could explain why the wilder Lamanites who dwelt along the coast were reported as "wandering about in the wilderness with [nothing but] a short skin girdle about their loins" [Enos 1:20].)

The climate and vegetation in the area where Lehi$_1$'s party first landed are not described in the Book of Mormon, but since the seeds the immigrants brought "did grow exceedingly" (1 Nephi 18:24), it is safe to assume both considerable heat and moisture. On the east sea coast, however, we learn that, at least during one season (on their new year's eve, in fact), the "heat of the day" was enough to cause "much fatigue" for marching warriors and an overpowering need to sleep (Alma 51:33). Of snow, ice, or cold in the land of promise, on the other hand, there is no hint anyplace in the text.

Two seasons are identified or implied. One is referred to as the "season of grain" (Helaman 11:6); this growing season would have been a time of rains. The other was a dry season. That was when wars were fought, men then being relatively free from farming tasks—while the weather was dry enough to permit travel and camping in the open.[40] This dual pattern is what one would expect in a tropical land.

Was the land fertile, naturally forested, desert, or what?

Tropical soils are typically not very fertile, because abundant rains wash away valuable nutrients. Certain areas in the Nephite and Lamanite lands would have been much richer in agricultural possibilities than others. Where rivers had deposited soils through flooding, in some flatter mountain valleys, and on the margins and deltas of rivers, substantial depth of good soil may occur. But in general the greenery of the vegetation in a tropical land is a more apparent than real sign of fertility, and cultivators using run-of-the-mill soil must change plots every few years to cope with declining fertility.

The unusual productivity that special areas could attain is seen in the local land of Zarahemla. Our knowledge of it comes from the account of the Nephites' battle with the Amlicites and Lamanites on the banks of the Sidon River. The combined enemy force, "so numerous that they could not be numbered" (Alma 2:35), were met and defeated by Alma₁ and his army on the west bank of the river. From there the Amlicites and Lamanites "fled before the Nephites towards the wilderness which was west and north" (Alma 2:36). In the melee, "many of their fields of grain were destroyed, for they were trodden down by the hosts of men" (Alma 3:2). Surprisingly, this loss caused actual famine for the inhabitants of the city and the local land of Zarahemla (see Alma 4:2–3). Evidently, the strip of cropland on rich alluvial soil next to the river Sidon, probably but a few miles in length, produced a substantial proportion of the community's food. Other Nephite settlements also seem to have been situated in depressions where streams likely left prime soil: a person went into or out of Gideon (see Alma 6:7), Melek (see Alma 8:3), Ammonihah (see Alma 15:1), Sidom (see Alma 15:1), and Manti (see Alma 43:22).

The picture we get of the land of Nephi, including the region around the city of Nephi and the lands of Shilom, Shemlon, Helam, Amulon, Ishmael, and so on, is of an extensive area of forested mountains or plateau country within which only certain valleys were settled. We can see this especially in the delight of Alma$_1$ and his group when they found the valley they called the land of Helam: "And they fled eight days' journey into the wilderness. And they came to a land, yea, even a very beautiful and pleasant land, a land of pure water" (Mosiah 23:3–4). This picture is confirmed in the accompanying narrative about the lost Lamanite army. From the city of Nephi, they chased after Limhi and his people, who had a head start trying to escape to Zarahemla. The pursuers lost the track after two days and then found they were "lost in the wilderness" (Mosiah 22:16; 23:30). After wandering about, they stumbled onto the people of Amulon, who had "begun to till the ground" in what they called the land of Amulon, a place the Lamanites had been unaware of (Mosiah 23:31). The Amulonites must not have liked pioneering much, because they abandoned their land to join with the Lamanites in trying to find a way back to Nephi. They still had no clue what route to take when they bumbled into Alma₁'s Helam (see Mosiah 23:31–37). In this instance and elsewhere in his comments or implications about the geography of Nephi, Mormon emphasizes how much wilderness there was. The picture conveyed is that relatively few areas of settlement existed amidst a virtual sea of forested, mountainous wilderness. (As noted earlier, we lack information from the Book of Mormon to assess how much long-range change in this picture might have been produced as a result of the great catastrophe described in 3 Nephi 8.)

The small plates of Nephi relate in Nephi₁'s words incidents in the Near East that give a different meaning of "wilderness." For example, in 1 Nephi 16 the word refers to desert. The basic meaning of the term translated from Hebrew as "wilderness" is apparently "uninhabited area," but when used in relation to the American promised land it may mean something different, because we read of wilderness that was "full of the Lamanites" (Alma 31:3; compare Alma 50:7, 9; 3 Nephi 3:17). In the New World, Lehi₁'s group immediately upon landing "journeyed in the wilderness," where they found "beasts in the forests of every kind" (1 Nephi 18:25). Bountiful, a lowland zone, was mostly "wilderness which is filled with all manner of wild animals of every kind" (Alma 22:31; compare Alma 2:37 on the wilderness of Hermounts). From the early land of Nephi, Enos "went to hunt beasts in the forests" (Enos 1:3), and at least patches of wilderness were found immediately adjacent to the city of Nephi in Zeniffite times (see Mosiah 10:9). Obviously, wilderness in these cases was in no sense desert, but probably forest. Limhi's explorers lost their way while headed to Zarahemla, probably because of the confusing, broken, forest-covered terrain they had to traverse (see Mosiah 8:8). Military movements through wilderness near Manti and elsewhere also make it clear that the wilderness consisted of forest, not open, barren space (see Alma 43:27–35; 58:18–19).

It is clear, then, that substantial areas of the land southward—probably most of it—were forested. When people went from that area to settle in the land northward, they encountered a marked contrast in the flora. Instead of the abundant timber resources that were at hand in their homelands southward, they now had to use alternative housing or import timber (see Helaman 3:7–10). Note too that the deforested portion of the land northward was not termed "wilderness," but merely "desolate" (Helaman 3:6).

What was the basis of economic life in the promised land?

The fundamental economic activity was farming: "They did raise grain in abundance, both in the north and in the south; and they did flourish exceedingly" (Helaman 6:12). Specific crops mentioned, at one point in time and in the land of Nephi, were "corn," "barley," "wheat," "neas," and "sheum," and "all manner of seeds" as well as fruits (Mosiah 9:9). "Corn" is intimated to have been the preferred grain (see Mosiah 7:22 and 9:9, where it is first in the list of grains, and Mosiah 9:14, according to which Lamanites stole it specifically). When grain was insufficient, famine prevailed (see Alma 3:2; 4:2; Helaman 11:5–6; 3 Nephi 4:3, 6). Nothing in the text suggests that the people prepared or cultivated the land using anything other than their own hands; while animals ("flocks and herds") were kept, they seem to have been used mainly for food (see, for example, 3 Nephi 3:22; 4:4).

Crop production under the best of conditions was abundant, sufficient to support a variety of craft workers (for example, see Helaman 6:11, 13) and to sustain a large number of administrative and other specialist personnel and an elite social class (see Mosiah 7:22; Alma 60:21–22; 3 Nephi 6:10–12). The economic surplus stimulated trade in both the lands southward and northward (see Mosiah 24:7; Helaman 3:10; 6:7–8). Some areas were productive enough to export a food surplus, while others ran short at times: central Zarahemla had to supply the Nephite army in the southwestern quarter of the land, for instance (see Alma 57:6; 58:4, 7), and the land of Melek was an exporter (see Alma 62:29).

Hunting was uncommon once the land had filled up with people and deprived the game of their natural habitat (see 3 Nephi 4:1–3). While hunting may have been an idealized traditional activity among the Lamanites, at least according to their biased Nephite neighbors (as in Enos 1:20), the high population level the Lamanites actually reached, as indicated by the size of their armies, cannot be accounted for except on the basis of settled agrarian living.[41]

What were some of the visible consequences of this economic system?

Mormon's economic view of his people was that prosperous conditions resulted when an ideal social and religious order was followed (for example, see Helaman 3:24, 25, 36; 4 Nephi 1:3, 23). Mormon felt that ideally the population should predominantly be cultivators and exhibit minimal distinctions in wealth (see Alma 32:4–5; 34:24–25; 35:9; 3 Nephi 6:1–5). Conversely, he believed that economic distress followed when the people became unrighteous and unequal. When such conditions arose, Mormon editorialized pointedly about the suffering and evils that resulted from differences in wealth and class distinctions (see Alma 4:6–9; 5:55; Helaman 3:36; 4:12; 6:39; 4 Nephi 1:26).

Mormon also had a sense of history on which he based his

understanding of changes in population and exploitation of the land. He knew that in early times the land was relatively empty (see in Mosiah 8:8 the story of Limhi's exploring party who missed finding the people at Zarahemla; see also Omni 1:13–14; Mosiah 23:30, 35). He exhibited satisfaction with stories of occupying new land and resulting prosperity (see Mosiah 23:19–20; Helaman 3:8; 11:20). In his own day, however, Mormon might not have cared much for the ecological and demographic realities that faced him. When he went south to Zarahemla as a youth, he observed, obviously impressed and perhaps a bit dismayed, that "the whole face of the land had become covered with buildings, and the people were as numerous almost, as it were the sand of the sea" (Mormon 1:7). Soon he was forced to lead his people as they scrambled to find refuge and subsistence in the land of Joshua and, after further flights, in Jashon, Shem, Desolation, Boaz, and who knows where else (see Mormon 2:6–7). His leadership experience in regard to economics and ecology must have been capped in the last few years before the climactic battle at the hill Cumorah. At that time he was responsible for a population of hundreds of thousands crowded together in the land of Cumorah (see Mormon 6:2–5, 10–15). Incidentally, the area must have had incredibly productive soil to have provisioned such a mass of people for the four years of their doomed stay.

The most visible consequence of Nephite economic practices would have been the widespread cultural modification of the landscape. Mormon and his predecessors knew that overpopulation could destroy an ecological system. He was struck with how the Jaredites who had preceded them had denuded the land of Desolation of all its trees (at least that is how the Nephites interpreted what they observed upon their arrival, although they may have overreacted; the land may have been naturally more treeless than they, who had come from forested country, considered natural). This treelessness was most visible in the land of Desolation, in or near where Mormon himself grew up. His own ancestors may have been among the Nephite colonists in the north who "did dwell in tents, and in houses of cement, and they did suffer whatsoever tree should spring up upon the face of the land that it should grow up, that in time they might have timber" (Helaman 3:9).

Such profound and widespread ecological, economic, and demographic consequences undoubtedly colored Mormon's mental map of the world in which he lived.

chapter 7

Civilization

The general question addressed in this chapter is, what elements of civilization mentioned in Mormon's record help us clarify his picture of Nephite geography?

Of course, the account is itself a manifestation of sophisticated ancient culture. The fact that there was such a record (which clearly fits into the category of ancient American codices)[42] argues that no simple tribe could have come up with such a book. It was part of a long tradition of record keeping. Its contents also report the civilized status of the makers of the record. The book records a history of a sometimes large population that lasted nearly a thousand years. Furthermore, statement after statement in the account documents that the Nephites participated in a genuine civilization.

We saw in chapter 3 that the promised land where Nephite history ran its course was conceived by the Nephites as an integral whole, a limited territory on the order of five hundred miles long and consisting of a pair of major lands on either side of an isthmus. The fact that they thought of that territory as a whole and represented it as a setting in which trade, warfare, and other intercommunication went on over centuries indicates that a single civilization was found there.

Since the Nephites and Lamanites were so often at war with each other, it may seem odd to speak of their being united in a single civilization, but there is good evidence to conclude that. Consider especially how often the two factions were in intimate contact with each other. To begin with, they came out of the same Jerusalem background. When Nephi$_1$ and Laman$_1$ were still alive, we are safe in supposing the culture their two groups shared was far greater than the ways in which they differed. Circumstances and preferences moved them farther apart as years went on, but at later times descendants of both groups were still close to each other in important ways. For example, the people of Ammon—Lamanites by birth and background—became Nephites formally and by loyalty and action. The Nephites were joined by other Lamanite refugees from time to time (see Alma 26:13–16; 35:6–9; 62:17). The reverse was also true. Dissenters from among the Nephites united with the Lamanites "from the reign of Nephi down to the ... time" of Amalickiah, according to Alma 47:35, and the process continued later. Mormon added the perceptive note, "Now these dissenters, [had] the same instruction and the same information [as] the Nephites" (Alma 47:36). They became rulers, commanders, and teachers among the Lamanites (for example, see Alma 24:1, 4–7; 43:6; 47:35; 48:1–6; Helaman 4:1–4). Note also how the religious "order and faith of Nehor" (Alma 14:16; see 1:15) inexplicably spread from the Nephites in the land of Zarahemla to Lamanite country in only a few years (see Alma 21:4). At certain times, too, many Lamanites resident in their homeland became believers in the Nephite religion. Some Lamanites came down among the Nephites to teach their cousins and even unite with them (see Helaman 5:50–51; 6:4–9; 3 Nephi 2:14–16; 3:14). Both Nephites and Lamanites colonized the land northward in peace (see Helaman 3:12–15), and at the end of Mormon's record the Nephites and Lamanites became equally evil and committed similarly heinous sins (see Moroni 9:8–9, 16, 19). In the final struggles and afterward, many Nephites were incorporated among the Lamanites (see Moroni 9:24). Thus we see that close relationships prevailed between Lamanite and Nephite societies despite the many conflicts, primarily between their leaders, that make it appear otherwise.

The disputes between the Nephites and Lamanites were largely over power—over which rulers would lead, and exploit, the mass of people. For instance, the bitter letters Moroni$_1$ and Ammoron exchanged (see Alma 54–55; Ammoron was not even a Lamanite, but a Nephite dissenter) are not about two different civilizations in conflict. They are about who will be in charge of the unified show.

Can conflict actually be a manifestation of a kind of unity? Wars between factions are now being recognized by some historians as evidence of a close relationship between the antagonists rather than a total separation. One scholarly analysis of civilization in relation to war recently concluded, "Conflict, hostility, and even warfare, when durable (habitual, protracted, or inescapable), are *forms of association* that create a social relationship between, and a social system composed of, the contestants, antagonists, and foes."[43] The author, political scientist David Wilkinson, argues that such rivals (in the case we are considering, Lamanites and Nephites) need each other as much as, say, the English and the Irish, opposing Hindu castes, or fighting spouses. Enmity actually helps the parties define their identities. In the Book of Mormon, the Nephites' and Lamanites' ways of life never diverged so drastically that they were wholly different entities; rather, the two groups were more like the yin and yang of a combined society.

So what were some of the features of their civilization that relate to geography? We shall consider aspects of urbanism, emblematic public constructions, government, warfare, literacy, religion, and systems of advanced knowledge, all of which influenced Mormon's formulation of the where, as much as the what, of his people's history.

Today, the presence of cities is crucial in how we rate the civilizational status of an area. What evidence does the Book of Mormon give for cities, and what was their geographical significance?

The Nephite record tells of a population that probably reached into the millions and was spread over hundreds of miles. Many cities are mentioned, and by all definitions a civilization constructs cities.[44] What did the Nephite cities signify about the centers of their population and the moving forces of their history?

The characteristics Nephite writers had in mind in defining a city are nowhere systematically discussed, but we can pick up allusions. When Mormon tells of the settlement of Helam by Alma$_1$ and his people, he reports that the little colony of only 450 souls (see Mosiah 18:35) started out planting crops, then built buildings, and followed by choosing Alma$_1$ as their formal leader. Shortly, when they began to prosper, "they built a city" that they called the city of Helam (Alma 23:20). A few years later when the Lamanite army entered the land, they surprised the men who were "in the city of Helam . . . tilling the land round about" (Alma 23:25). A city as defined by the Nephites thus did not have to involve a population beyond a few hundred. Furthermore, part of the territory constituting the city could still be cultivated. At a far extreme, however, a city could have a large population: Moroni$_1$'s charge of neglect by the central government headed by Pahoran$_1$ speaks of the leaders in the city of Zarahemla living among "thousands" and even "tens of thousands" of people who "sit in idleness," either in the capital city or in the land immediately about it (Alma 60:22).

Several types, or levels, of Nephite cities are identified. A type of city that was sometimes small was the military garrison city that was established quickly. Antiparah, Zeezrom, and Cumeni, which all lay between Manti and the west sea, were of this sort (see Alma 50:10–11; 56:9–10, 13–16). More of these "instant cities" were installed near the east sea coast (see Alma 50:13–15). (They are reminiscent of the small fortified settlements, or even isolated fortresses, that existed in Old Testament times in the land of Israel but were labeled cities in the Bible because they were surrounded by defensive walls.)[45] Another type of city was isolated and had little or no surrounding land under its control (for example, Lemuel and Shimnilom in Alma 23:12 and perhaps Boaz, Shem, Jashon, and Jordan in Mormon 2–5). Still another kind of city served as an administrative and probably commercial and ritual center that governed smaller places and surrounding land (for example, note the phrase "who were in all the regions round about" [Alma 22:27]; the city of Lehi administered the city of Morianton, according to Alma 50:36). The crowning class of urban settlement was the "great city." Six Nephite cities and one Jaredite city are named, and others existed but are not named in the record (see Helaman 7:22; 8:5–6; 3 Nephi 8:14; 10:2; Ether 10:20). As to the size of Nephite cities, note that the city of Jerusalem in Israel was called a "great city,"[46] and Nazareth in Galilee was considered a "city" (1 Nephi 11:13) even though its population was only in the hundreds, according to archaeological data.[47]

By the time Mormon was a youth, after A.D. 300, the Nephites had built or rebuilt so many cities and towns that "the whole . . . land had become covered with buildings" (Mormon 1:7). That was more or less true along the corridor through which the young man traveled from the land northward to Zarahemla, although obviously, other ecological areas would have had little or no such buildup.

The text's characterization of urban settlements in Nephite and Lamanite territory definitely justifies applying the label civilization. The most consequential lands were those that contained the most cities. Moreover, that the Nephite record refers to cities on this scale indicates that archaeological evidence of ancient cities ought to be apparent in whatever part of the New World was the actual scene of their lands.

Does Mormon's book talk about the Nephites carrying out major building projects?

One would expect large public buildings and other structures to be built in conjunction with cities. A complete picture of Nephite geography considers the distribution of temples, towers, palaces, fortifications, and roads as evidences of the power of the rulers.

Let us begin with the earliest Nephites, headed by founder Nephi$_1$. When they separated from the faction headed by Laman$_1$ and Lemuel, they settled in a place they called Nephi. The colonizing party proceeded to build a temple modeled after the temple of Solomon in Jerusalem (see 2 Nephi 5:16). The new structure could not have been very large (only half a dozen Nephite men were on hand to construct it),[48] yet the people and their ruler, Nephi$_1$, must have considered such a building essential if their little kingdom was to have political and religious standing, even in their own eyes. Later they walled in the city (see Mosiah 9:8). Aside from its practical value, the wall also demonstrated that this first band of Nephites considered themselves a significant people.

The pattern of a people constructing its political identity through public building projects was also demonstrated by the Zeniffites, an offshoot of the Nephites. Their king, Noah, built a "spacious palace" (Mosiah 11:9) and refurbished the city's old temple complex internally and by adding "a tower near the temple; yea, a very high tower" (Mosiah 11:12). Atop a hill near the city, Noah also built a "great tower" (Mosiah 11:13). In Book of Mormon usage, "tower" relates back to the "great tower" that was built, according to Genesis 11, in the land of Shinar, or Mesopotamia (see Ether 1:3, 5, 33), and is commonly referred to as "the tower of Babel." This type of tower was a ziggurat, a sacred artificial mountain where heavenly beings were believed to dwell or visit.[49] Among Nephites and Lamanites, towers like those that Noah erected were marks of an influential community, and the structures served as rallying points for local governments (see Alma 48:1). Like European cathedrals, towers asserted the renown and political power of the community. Accordingly, when Captain Moroni set out to subdue the king-men, who had defied the authority of the Nephite government (see Alma 51:7–8, 13, 17), he "did pull down their pride and their nobility" by slaying thousands of them (Alma 57:18–19). The defeated survivors of the movement were then "compelled to hoist the title [flag] of liberty upon their towers, and in their cities" as a sign of submission (Alma 51:20). Obviously, any settlement deserving to be labeled a city would have had a tower, and larger cities might have had many. The ability of a ruler to muster manpower and organize resources to construct a tower—the bigger the better—communicated his administrative ability, power, and glory. There were also towers of ritual significance built and controlled by kin groups or families (see Helaman 7:10–14).

Towers existed throughout Nephite history. Mormon wrote to his son Moroni$_2$ in the final years of the Nephite wars about conditions facing their people at "the tower of Sherrizah," presumably a landmark somewhere in the land northward that needed no further identification (Moroni 9:7; see 9:16–17). We do not know how towers related to "churches," a later type of public building, but some sort of connection is possible. Following the Savior's appearance to the people at the city Bountiful, the twelve disciples "formed a church of Christ in all the lands round about" (4 Nephi 1:1). After approximately A.D. 200, that unified ecclesiastical pattern was modified, "and they began to build up churches unto themselves to get gain" (4 Nephi 1:26) under "many priests and false prophets" (4 Nephi 1:34). By the middle of that century, "they did still continue to build up churches unto themselves, and adorn them with all manner of precious things" (4 Nephi 1:41). The switch in meaning of "church" from an organizational entity to a physical structure is not further clarified.

In addition to discussing temples, towers, and churches, the Nephite record mentions "palace" constructions (Mosiah 11:9; Alma 22:2) in key capital cities, although we are given no details about the nature of such buildings.

Fortifications were still another way to publicly display the power of a people and its rulers while impacting the landscape. Moroni$_1$ caused his men to "commence in digging up heaps of earth round about all the cities" in Zarahemla (Alma 50:1). These were topped with log palisades (see Alma 50:6). The constructions, along with other military measures that Moroni$_1$

initiated, gave his people "assurance of protection" (Alma 50:12). Beyond the practical benefit of providing a safe haven in case of enemy attack, the successful construction of the fortifications demonstrated to folks whose morale may have been wavering that they were led by a decisive regime that they could trust. That is part of the psychology behind all massive public works, and such public works are essential in a civilization.

Wherever the Nephites dwelt, they would have constructed public works projects, small or great. The record we have makes clear that it was part of their civilizational pattern to do so. Mormon's thinking about the geography of his people would have been punctuated by images in his mind of some notable structures they had built. Again, in the area where they lived we should find archaeological remains of what the Book of Mormon calls temples, towers, churches, palaces, and fortifications.

Trade and large-scale war are other features considered essential aspects of a civilization. What does the Book of Mormon say about those?

Little is reported about merchants and their activities over much of Nephite history, but at a few points in the Book of Mormon account we read of extensive commerce. It is impossible that a civilization that included widespread trade and related components—record keeping, craft production, knowledge of routes, and so on—would have arisen suddenly at just those moments. The pattern must have been going on for a long time, becoming particularly visible when it reached a climax level. Helaman 6:7–8 reports at about the time of Christ, "The Nephites did go into whatsoever part of the land they would, whether among the Nephites or the Lamanites. And . . . the Lamanites did also go whithersoever they would . . . ; and thus they did have free intercourse one with another, to buy and to sell, and to get gain." (Third Nephi 6:8, 12 imply the same thing.) Around A.D. 300, "gold and silver did they lay up in store in abundance, and did traffic in all manner of traffic" (4 Nephi 1:46). So the civilization in which the Nephites and Lamanites participated engaged in substantial trade by which some people became "exceedingly rich" (Alma 50:18; 4 Nephi 1:23). Mormon, as one of the elite class among the Nephite people in his day, may well have learned a great deal about areas that he had not personally visited through merchants who had traveled about more widely.

As for warfare as a characteristic of civilization, the Nephite record is so detailed about their highly developed patterns of fighting that there is no need to spell out particulars. Armies of tens of thousands and even hundreds of thousands are reported.[50] This reflects the large-scale population of Book of Mormon peoples, and the targets of aggression and defense signal to us, as to Mormon, the critical spots vital to the maintenance of the Nephites' national being and territory. A civilization involves large-scale wars, big armies, and terrible destruction; thus the society we see in Mormon's record indeed qualifies as "civilized," paradoxical as that may seem.

Because religion was of great importance to the Nephites, would not Mormon's sense of the boundaries of his own territory have been influenced by what he perceived to be the area within which religious beliefs and practices familiar to him, or closely related to his, prevailed?

This is a reasonable proposition. The Book of Mormon characterizes the peoples whose history it treats (Nephites, Lamanites, Mulekites, and Jaredites) as for the most part sharing, or at least being familiar with, features that we consider elements of religion: a supreme god or gods, the use of sacred books, prophecies and their fulfillment according to a calendar, priests, temples, sacrifices, altars, prayers, oaths, sacred festivals, inspiration via the Spirit, belief in resurrection, and so on. The Book of Mormon prophets and writers assumed these elements to be givens in religion. To be sure, those elite record keepers had their own version of the general pattern that differed in significant details from what others accepted; nevertheless, all the Nephites, and no doubt many of the Mulekites and Lamanites, were familiar with the basic scheme of belief and practices. (In the same way, Catholics, Protestants, Mormons, and Jews know the broad elements of their shared religious tradition—enough to criticize each other—but they are not able to compare themselves in the same way with, say, Buddhists.) Many Lamanites were familiar enough with the Nephite religious tradition that they could adopt it (see, for example, Alma 18).

In short, those living in and around the promised land were broadly united by the cultural patterns behind a shared religious life. This seems to indicate that the Book of Mormon peoples participated in one civilization, in contrast to differently configured patterns of religion evident in other civilizational areas.

Wouldn't Nephite country also show evidence of writing and books?

Indeed so. Mormon was aware that his predecessors kept "many books and many records of every kind" (Helaman 3:15), and large numbers of those records were in his people's archive, which he controlled. But how might records have influenced Mormon's geographic vision?

In the first place, the brass plates—approximately equivalent to our Old Testament—had been brought from old

Jerusalem. They provided background for Mormon to understand what Nephi$_1$ had prophesied in 1 Nephi 11–14 about world history, so to speak. That is, from the Nephite records, Mormon gained an intercontinental perspective on the history and geography of his people. From the brass plates, plus the accounts of earlier Nephite and Jaredite prophets and the words of the Savior to the Nephites, Mormon also understood certain key events and influences in the ancient Near East, the ministry and death of the Savior there, the historical past and prophetic future of the Jewish Jerusalem as well as the New Jerusalem to come, and the gospel restoration that would come a millennium and half after his day. Thus his view was not simply of the tribal territory of his Nephite ancestors, but of the worldwide scene.

A second point about the presence of books among Book of Mormon peoples is that they point us, as do the archaeological remains of cities mentioned earlier, toward a particular area in the New World where the lands of the Nephites must have been located.

Does that mean that what we might call advanced knowledge about the natural world, or science, was limited to the same area?

Not entirely. The most advanced knowledge of astronomy and the calendar in the Americas occurred in Mesoamerica (Mexico and Guatemala), yet in Peru and Bolivia the ancient cultures knew considerable about those subjects. In fact, some of the peoples in the New World whose cultural level was not generally as high as that of those in the Mesoamerican and Andean areas still had significant knowledge of the heavenly bodies. The knowledge possessed by South American peoples was not as elaborate as what the northerners knew, and the apparent lack of written records anywhere on the southern continent prevented the peoples there from accumulating as many detailed observations and calculations as did those in Mexico and Guatemala.

According to the Book of Mormon, the Nephites knew that the planets circled the sun (see Helaman 12:15). They also used multiple interlocking calendars (see, for example, 3 Nephi 1:1; 2:8).[51] While he was still a youth, Mormon began "to be learned somewhat after the manner of the learning" of his people (Mormon 1:2), so it would not be surprising if then or later he controlled some of his group's "higher knowledge," such as their calendars and astronomy. In any case, he was no doubt aware that such expertise existed among men in his civilization.

The particulars of that advanced knowledge would have set apart the civilization in which Mormon was involved from any others he may have known about. A man as influential and extensively traveled as Mormon was—he was chief military commander over upwards of a million people for much of his adult life—might have encountered a number of representatives of other cultures, such as merchants. He also knew of other cultures from the records in his hands (see Mormon 9:32–33). His son Moroni$_2$ observed that "none other people knoweth our language" (Mormon 9:34), which suggests that he was aware of other tongues.

With these perspectives, it seems plausible that Mormon understood the uniqueness of his civilization, not only its literacy, books, literature, calendars, astronomical knowledge, and so on, but also its unique geographical setting. If that is true, it may help explain why he was not interested in cultures outside the Nephite/Lamanite area, even though he was aware that they existed. (This willful ignorance may be similar to that of the Chinese, who considered their ways so superior that they were contemptuous of all surrounding cultures or civilizations.)

chapter 8

*H*istorical Geography

The sequence of cultures in a land, with their changing centers of development and influence, gives us another dimension of geography. For example, a full characterization of the geography of the United States requires understanding that comes only through a set of successive maps each related to a date or period: discovery, early colonists, the colonies at the time of the American Revolution, the westward expansion, the Civil War, urbanization, and so on. Maps of key changes in population and activity over time dynamically explain not only the what and when, but even the why, of any area's course of development.

We have enough information on the Nephites' expansion to sketch out its main lines, but for certain geographical areas within their promised land, as well as for certain historical periods, our information remains slim. In the case of the Lamanites we know their history even less well. Mormon, of course, was aware of much more detail about both peoples than we can know, but whether he systematically thought through the historical geography of the promised land is a question we cannot answer. But he must have had rudiments of a time-sequenced picture in his mind, whether or not he or anybody else among his people ever framed it definitively.

What was the geographical setting for the earliest era of Nephite and Lamanite history?

This historical period begins with the landing of Lehi₁'s party and continues to the migration of Mosiah₁ to Zarahemla (see 1 Nephi 18:23–Omni 1:13). Of course, we have this information only from the small plates of Nephi, not through Mormon. The historical and geographical data accessible is cryptic, and we are left to infer much.

The events covered include the separation of Nephi₁ and his group from those led by Laman₁ and Lemuel, who remained in the land of first inheritance; the settlement in the land of Nephi; local geographical expansion by the Nephites; Lamanite pressure on the Nephites; and finally, the departure of Mosiah₁ and his party to Zarahemla.

Chapter 5 discussed the movement of Nephi₁'s original party from the coastal land of first inheritance up to the land of Nephi. Once there they "waxed strong in the land," "multiplied exceedingly, and spread upon the face of the land" (Jarom 1:5, 8). These descriptions of growth must be read cautiously: only about five adult males were in the original Nephite party, so even after several centuries the population would still have been tiny, unless they had incorporated "native" people into their social and political system (this is, in fact, probable).[52] Since they were occasionally attacked by the Lamanites, they would have hesitated to extend to more distant places except in substantial numbers, which they did not have. (When the Zeniffites came to the land of Nephi several centuries later, they repaired the walls of two former Nephite cities, Lehi-Nephi and Shilom. The original Nephites probably had never spread beyond the local land around those two settlements [see Mosiah 9:8], and the Lamanites had only lightly, and thus recently, inhabited the two lands [see Mosiah 9:6–7].)

The earliest Lamanites, meanwhile, inhabited wilderness along the west sea coast. If they subsisted by any means other than hunting and foraging at this stage, there is no hint of it in the text, yet their population growth at least kept pace with that of the Nephites. The Lamanites probably also incorporated other groups. For their earliest positions, see map 12.

By a generation after 300 B.C., "the more wicked part of the Nephites were destroyed" (Omni 1:5). The implication is that this destruction was a result of wars with the Lamanites. The extreme brevity of the small plates regarding this period makes our view of the history especially sketchy, but around 200 B.C. Mosiah$_1$ was "warned of the Lord that he should flee out of the land of Nephi, and as many as would hearken . . . should also depart out of the land with him" (Omni 1:12). Whether Mosiah$_1$ was a ruler in Nephi before his departure is left unsaid, but he carried with him the records on metal plates and the sacred artifacts that would have been kept by the Nephite king. Nothing more is said about those Nephites who remained behind; presumably they were exterminated, although some might have survived to mix with the Lamanites. Mosiah$_1$ and his fellow refugees "were led by many preachings and prophesyings" through the wilderness "until they came down into the land which is called the land of Zarahemla" (Omni 1:13).

Where were the people of Zarahemla, or Mulekites, located before Mosiah$_1$'s arrival among them?

Mulek's party are said to have landed first in the land northward (see Alma 22:30; Helaman 6:10), then at least some

MAP 12. EARLY SPREAD OF MAJOR GROUPS

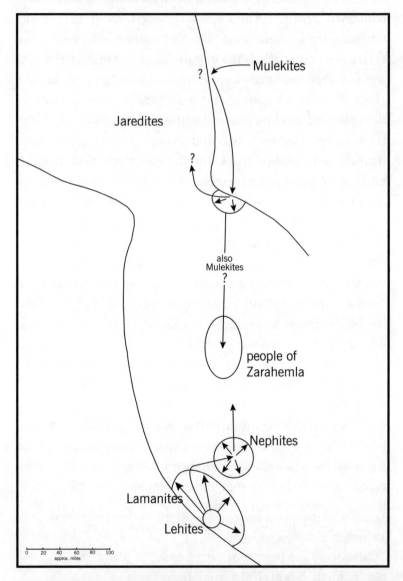

The early immigrant groups did not multiply and spread out quickly or far.
For centuries they remained mostly apart from each other, as though on
settled "islands" amid a "sea" of wilderness.

of their descendants later "came from there up into the [then] south wilderness" (Alma 22:31) to the land of Zarahemla, where Mosiah₁ found them. The text of the Book of Mormon refers to a place called "the city of Mulek" (Alma 51:26) near the east coast, but it does not indicate how the city originated. It is reasonable to assume that the city was named after "him [Mulek] who first possessed" that place, in accordance with later Nephite custom (Alma 8:7). Probably the first settlement of those who arrived from the Mediterranean with Mulek's party was at this place near the east sea. Inasmuch as subsequent history mentions that the party's descendants "had many wars and serious contentions, and [their having] fallen by the sword from time to time" (Omni 1:17), we could suppose that internal conflicts gradually pushed one portion of the Mulekites, the people of Zarahemla, up the Sidon River to the area where Mosiah₁ found them. (See map 13.) Others of the original population in the east coastal lowlands may have remained there or spread upriver through the intermediate area; that makes more sense than the Zarahemla group constituting the sole survivors who for no apparent reason vaulted up the river in one movement.[53] (I suspect that "the people who were in the land Bountiful" mentioned in Alma 50:32 as a loyalty concern to Moroni₁ were of the same origin, remotely, as the people of Zarahemla. The text gives no hint of a Nephite colonization before the time of the statement.)

What was the geography of the Zeniffite enclave among the Lamanites in Nephi?

Zeniff's deal with the Lamanite king was that the Zeniffites could occupy the two local lands originally called Nephi and Shilom (under the Lamanites, Nephi was renamed Lehi-Nephi). While their population initially grew modestly, over time casualties from battling the Lamanites reduced their numbers drastically (see Mosiah 21:17). Map 11 highlights the small zone the Zeniffites occupied.

How did the Lamanites expand their territory?

Once the Zeniffites under King Limhi escaped their over-lords, the Lamanites spread from their west lowland home base up through the lands of Shemlon and Shilom to Nephi proper. By the time the sons of Mosiah$_2$ and their companions arrived in the land of Nephi some thirty years later, the Lamanite king was established in the city of Lehi-Nephi and his people occupied the surrounding lands (see Alma 20:1; 22:1). The Book of Mormon indicates that the lands of Helam and Amulon were later incorporated in the Lamanite domain (see Mosiah 23:1–5, 25–35). The Lamanites also controlled a new city, Jerusalem, and had settled the lands of Ishmael and Middoni (see Alma 17:19; 20:4; 21:1–2). Further, the Lamanite king exercised some degree of rule over other lands as distant as both the east and west sea coasts (see Alma 22:27). Whether ethnic Lamanites physically spread to those lands or whether locals in the most distant of those places only symbolically affiliated themselves with the rulership of the king in Lehi-Nephi we cannot tell. In any case, in the second century B.C. the total population sub-servient to the Lamanite king grew rapidly in a short period of time. Map 13 shows the expansion of Nephite and Lamanite settlement between about 200 and 50 B.C.

MAP 13. EXPANSION OF NEPHITES AND LAMANITES IN THE TIME OF THE TWO ALMAS
By the lifetimes of the sons of Mosiah$_2$ and Moroni$_1$, the population ruled by the Lamanite kings occupied the highland Nephi area and reached from sea to sea. Nephite groups had spread throughout the Sidon basin and into Bountiful.

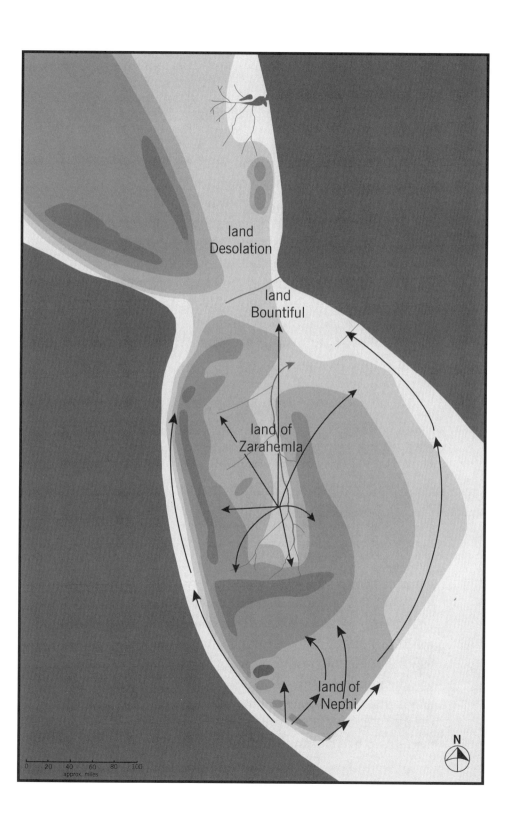

Where were the scenes of the lengthy war started by Amalickiah?

Amalickiah's strategy for conquering the Nephites was apparently set by his Zoramite advisors (see Alma 48:5), who had some traditional role among Nephite military forces that is not entirely clear but that made them privy to vital information.[54] Four attack routes were possible: (1) along the short east coast to capture the narrow neck and thus surround the Nephites, (2) hitting the southwest sector west of Manti to get at the city of Zarahemla, (3) moving northward along the west coast and over into Ammonihah, and (4) hitting the center of the land, Zarahemla, in a frontal assault via Manti. Amalickiah tried the first three, but the fourth was not tried until a quarter century later (see Helaman 1:19).

The strategically preferred plan called for an overwhelming offensive to be launched toward the narrow neck from the Zoramite homeland, Antionum, on the east sea coast area (see Alma 51:22–29). That place was the Lamanites' base nearest the vital isthmus (see Alma 50:32; 52:9). The attacks on Nephite outposts on the south and west part of the land of Zarahemla—from Manti to Antiparah—were apparently not considered to have much chance of success but were largely diversionary (see Alma 56:13–15, 20, 24–26). The attack that proceeded down the west coast of Nephite territory to strike at Ammonihah was a long shot (see Alma 16:2–3, 9; 49:1–25). The distance involved put the Lamanite strike force well beyond any hope of support from the homeland. If they failed, they failed, but they just might strike it lucky.

The important thing to know about this historical situation is that the movements were based on a well-thought-out strategy. They did not result from some imaginative scheme thought up by amateurs. Mormon, an experienced strategist, could see this as he studied the historical records, and he surely appreciated the full significance of what was going on in the battle of strategies between the Lamanite-Zoramite general staff and Captain Moroni, as shown by comments like that in Alma 50:32.

In what parts of the land northward did colonists from the land southward settle?

This topic has already been discussed but is recapitulated and extended here to draw attention to an important historical episode. The parts of the land northward where the Nephites lived (the "north countries" of Ether 1:1) were those they tried to defend the most desperately in Mormon's last campaigns. They were the same zones from which people were gathered around A.D. 25, according to 3 Nephi 3–4, to a refuge area in the land southward to wait out the robbers. The northern limits of focused Nephite colonization did not extend much beyond the land of Cumorah; all the surviving Nephites could collect there in the fourth century A.D. despite the social chaos resulting from a string of defeats at the hands of the Lamanites (see Mormon 5–6). Map 14 shows the probable routes of Nephite expansion into the land northward.

The question of where migrants of Lamanite extraction settled in the land northward is, however, unclear (see Helaman 3:12). They might have gone to areas other than "the north country" in the eastern lowlands.

Nearly all the information about colonization of the land northward comes from the first century B.C. Information later in the Book of Mormon is minimal. After the virtual geographic silence of 4 Nephi, we read of Mormon living around A.D. 300 in the land northward, where he apparently lived all his young life (see Mormon 1:1–5). The Nephites are there

MAP 14. NEPHITE EXPANSION INTO THE LAND NORTHWARD

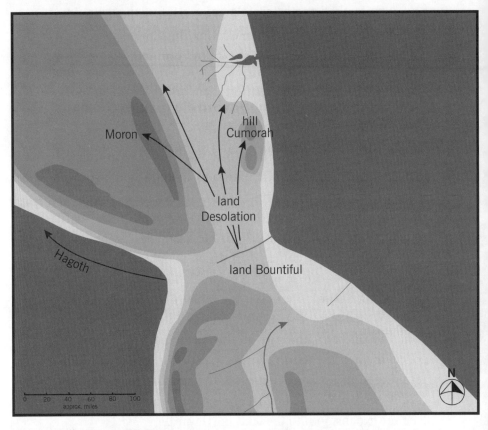

Hagoth built a few ships to sail to land northward colonies, but apparently most migrants went overland via the land Desolation.

without historical comment; most likely Mormon's ancestors had arrived there over three centuries earlier in one of the movements described in the book of Helaman.

The center of gravity of the Nephite population moved quietly northward between 50 B.C. and A.D. 30. In earlier centuries, first Nephi and then Zarahemla were the key Nephite centers. By around 40 B.C. the Nephites temporarily found it necessary to retreat well northward, to the land of Bountiful and even farther north (see Helaman 4), but they soon regained control of their traditional homeland in the land of Zarahemla. Each northbound shift probably left behind a residue of Nephites who chose to build new lives there. The northward shift of the population is particularly evident in the Savior's visit to the people in the city Bountiful (see 3 Nephi 11:1). All the disciples he chose at that time to lead his church were already living at Bountiful, and it was there that he established the headquarters, as it were, of the church. Nephi and Zarahemla were no longer central and perhaps not even significant. From that point on, events centered on the isthmus—the geographic feature that united the lands northward and southward. When young Mormon left his home area, which lay somewhere near or in the hill section that included Cumorah, and was taken to Zarahemla, he was touring the central Nephite zone.

Still, only a part of the land northward was of concern. Not a single hint in the topographic references involving the Nephite possessions in the land northward points to any highland territory; there are no "ups" or "downs" in Mormon's personal account that relate to the northern lands themselves. Nothing suggests that the Nephites settled or dwelt in the Jaredites' Moron, which was "up." The hills Shim and Cumorah (and clearly there would have been some others around) are referred to, but no mountains.

Which parts of the land do we know were damaged by the great natural disaster at the time of the Savior's death?

The account of the Savior's visit to Bountiful tells us that while there was indeed noteworthy damage inflicted by storms, winds, earthquakes, and perhaps volcanism (see 3 Nephi 11:1), life quickly returned to a semblance of normality. The worst of the destruction missed at least Bountiful (twenty-five hundred people gathered around the temple for some occasion, and they were not without food and homes).

The Lord's account of destroyed cities tells a story of great damage. The listing of their fates (see 3 Nephi 8–9) informs us of sixteen named cities that bore the brunt of the natural catastrophe. The list appears to be in two parts: 3 Nephi 9:3–7 gives the names of three destroyed places that we know were located in the land southward, so it is logical that the four cities mentioned with them were also located in the south. Verses 8–10 form a distinct segment of text and probably name cities farther northward. Jacobugath was farther north than all the other cities mentioned in the Book of Mormon for which we know locations. Very likely the others mentioned with it in these three verses were likewise to the north.

Map 15 indicates the location of cities for which we know or can infer a position. Other cities, whose positions we are uncertain about, I have placed at random in either the land southward or land northward, as implied in the previous paragraph (except for Moronihah; the Nephite military leader Moronihah operated in the borders by the east sea around Jershon, and the city named for him quite certainly was there also).

Where did the Nephites finally retreat from and to?

First the Nephites were driven to Joshua from the Zarahemla area through a land called at that time David, as well as from a city known as Angola (see Mormon 2). The probable course of their retreat is shown on map 16.

MAP 15. POSSIBLE DISTRIBUTION OF CITIES DESTROYED ACCORDING TO 3 NEPHI 8–9
We know where a few of the stricken cities named in the Lord's disaster account lay. On the basis of names of other cities listed with those few, a distribution something like this seems reasonable.

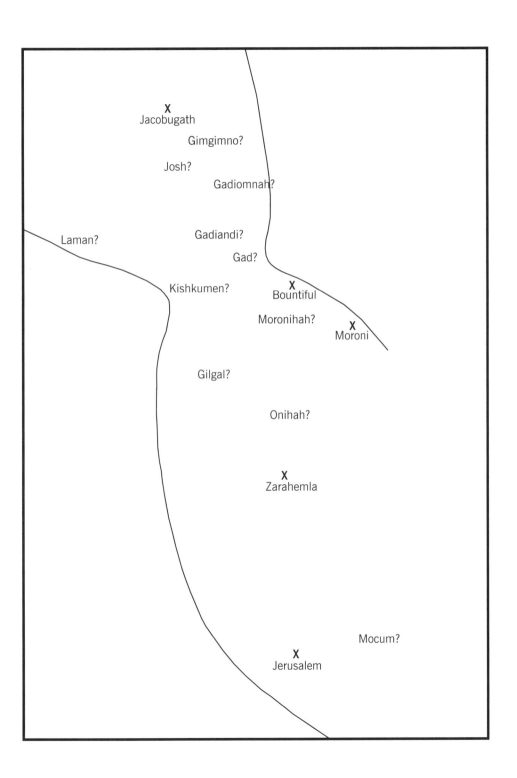

MAP 16. FINAL FLIGHT OF THE NEPHITES FROM THE LAND SOUTHWARD

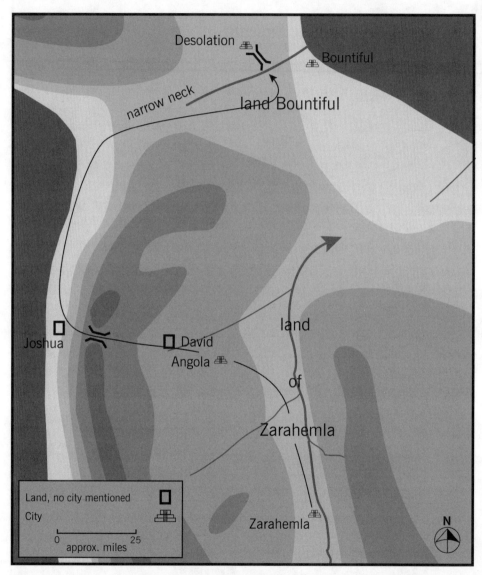

Mormon's account is too brief to give us a full picture, but at least the main body of Nephites followed this route in their final retreat from the land of Zarahemla.

North of the narrow pass two historical episodes of retreat occurred. An early rout sent the Nephites reeling all the way to Jashon, which was near the hill Shim (see Mormon 2:16–17). They recovered from this loss to the extent of even retaking the land of Zarahemla (see Mormon 2:27), but they had already demonstrated that they could not defend that large territory. They took advantage of their temporary good fortune in winning back their land southward territory and traded the indefensible land for hoped-for stability. They made a treaty with their enemies that established a new boundary between the parties at the narrow neck (see Mormon 2:28–29). The agreement lasted for some years, until the old ethnic hatred aroused a new war (see Mormon 3:1–4).

Eventually the Nephites were driven northward anew (see Mormon 4:19–5:7). This time there would be no further chance for political redemption. In a last gamble, they chanced everything on one climactic battle at the hill Cumorah (see Mormon 6:1–6). That slaughter marked the end of the Nephites as a people. The final wars are documented geographically on map 17.

Underlying the Nephite-Lamanite historical picture were always the mysterious Jaredites. King Mosiah$_1$'s subjects were "desirous beyond measure to know concerning those people who had been destroyed" (Mosiah 28:12; see 8:12). They felt powerfully that the desolated place where millions had preceded them in death was under a "great curse" (3 Nephi 3:24).

This sketch of the historical movements of the Nephites and other Book of Mormon groups teaches two things: (1) The lands described in physical terms in previous chapters went through a series of changes in the peoples, and presumably the cultures, that occupied them between the sixth century B.C. and the fourth century A.D. Those developments and events

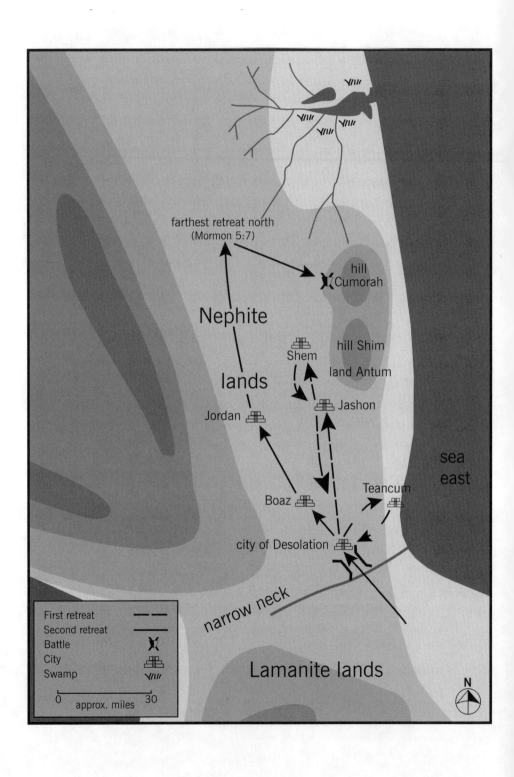

ought to be manifested in the archaeological remains, art, and linguistic history of whatever area was the actual place where the events took place. (2) Mormon, Moroni$_2$, and other writers of the Book of Mormon held in their minds as part of their geographical picture notions derived from that historical sequence.

MAP 17. FINAL WARS IN THE LAND NORTHWARD
The retreats and advances of Nephite and Lamanite armies in the final decades before the Nephites' extinction took place in the same restricted area where the Jaredites last fought.

chapter 9

S o How Much Do We Know?

After sifting through the text of the Book of Mormon in search of geographical information, as we have just done, we end up with what I call "Mormon's Map." The meaning of that label is that our graphic representation is, in large part, a simplified two-dimensional rendering of the body of information about geography that Mormon possessed in his mind.

We must, of course, say "simplified" and add "partial" for two reasons: (1) even Mormon could not have recalled at the time he was writing all the knowledge he had acquired about the lands he personally traversed (we ourselves "know" things geographical from our personal experiences that we never could express in words); and (2) Mormon drew on what he knew of geography and shed light on those matters only when it seemed required in order to formulate his account based for the most part on records kept by others. He wanted to teach moral lessons to future readers, not instruct them about sheer facts of history and geography. Geography was significant for his task at some points, but not central to it.

It would be absurd to assume that the incomplete map we have been able to deduce from the text represents all that our author-editor could tell us if he were sitting by our side as a consultant on geography. We have been able to derive from his record only an approximation, yet it is a reasonable approximation. It utilizes all the information I have been able to elicit from Mormon's words and those of other Book of Mormon writers. It is remarkably consistent and provides an enlightening setting for events reported in the record. No doubt this version can be improved, and will be if we discover new points in the text of the Book of Mormon that require change in the map.

Because of lack of explicit information, at points I have had to make assumptions, whereas Mormon probably had recorded or observed facts to fill my informational gaps. By what route and how far did Alma's people travel from Mormon to Helam? I try to answer that question by seeking examples from the travel accounts that seem to tell of journeys under somewhat similar circumstances. My assumptions are subject to correction, but they are the best I can do at present.

The map we have at this point is perhaps like those maps of parts of the Americas that European cartographers made in the sixteenth and seventeenth centuries. They drew in coastlines on the basis of reports that were not very clear or full from voyagers who had traversed portions of the coast. Where they did not possess direct information, those mapmakers made inferences—guesses may be more accurate. As for the interior spaces beyond the coasts, their information was even sketchier. Still, the maps they drafted were avidly sought by later voyagers and served them well enough. The comprehensive "Mormon's Map" on the inside front cover of this book can prove useful too.

To what uses can a map in this tentative condition be put?

I see three services this map can furnish:

1. It gives us a model that we can apply to stories from the record to check their consistency and perhaps shed new light on factors they involved that had not occurred to us before (and maybe not even to Mormon).
2. From the map we may discern new questions about geography—that is, see gaps in our knowledge for which we might seek answers by consulting Mormon's text anew.
3. The map summarizes a set of criteria, discussed in chapters 2–8, against which to evaluate proposals for where in the external world Nephite lands were located.

As examples of the first type of exercise, consider these questions: Why did the Lamanites, after slaying many of their fellow Lamanites who were converted by the sons of Mosiah$_2$, swear vengeance on the Nephites, whom they then attacked at a distant and unlikely spot, the land of Ammonihah (see Alma 25:1–2)? Or can we see from geography why Captain Moroni feared that the people in Bountiful might ally themselves with Morianton in the land of waters to the north to form a political entity that would have dire consequences for the Nephites (see Alma 50:29–32)? And why did the Lamanites consent to give Mormon and the Nephites four years to prepare for the battle at Cumorah? Why didn't they attack them immediately, while they were weakened (see Mormon 6:1–3)?

Regarding the second function, we might want to know what conditions of geography in the intermediate area gave Amalickiah the freedom and confidence to move his armies unperturbed over three hundred miles, from the land of Nephi to near the Nephite city of Moroni, in preparation for launching his blitzkrieg attack (see Alma 51:11–14, 22). What was, or was not, in the area between Nephi and the east sea?

The third use may help us sort through a vast amount of LDS effort that has been expended over more than a century. In my 1992 work, *The Geography of Book of Mormon Events: A Source Book,* I tabulated and summarized scores of theories of Book of Mormon geography that have been put forward by students of the topic. The flood of new and duplicative theories has not been stemmed by the failure of any previous ones to convince others of their accuracy.

In one section of that 1992 book, I arranged a "report card" for evaluating proposed relations between the real world and Book of Mormon lands. More than 110 criteria were listed. One could rate any theory with an A, B, C, D, or F grade according to how well it met the criteria set out for us by Mormon's record. For instance, if a particular theory proposed that the distance from Nephi to Zarahemla was either fifty miles or one thousand miles, it should receive an F grade on that point. Nobody seems to have taken my report card seriously, but it still offers a path through the jungle of mistaken information and bad logic that has for so long plagued geographical study of the Book of Mormon.

The features found on "Mormon's Map" as presented in this book are more carefully defined, more logically cross-checked, and more numerous than the criteria in the 1992 work. It should now be possible to evaluate confidently the theories that have been presented according to how well they agree with or fail to match the map that Mormon had in his mind. To perform those evaluations is a task for another time and place, but now, at least, the task is feasible because we have a view into Mormon's mind.

Notes

1. Joseph Smith, *History of the Church of Jesus Christ of Latter-day Saints,* ed. B. H. Roberts (Salt Lake City: Deseret News, 1946), 4:461.

2. *Discourses of Brigham Young,* ed. John A. Widtsoe (Salt Lake City: Deseret Book, 1941), 128.

3. See Lynn C. Layton, "An 'Ideal' Book of Mormon Geography," *The Improvement Era* 41 (July 1938): 394–95, 439.

4. See Ezra Taft Benson, "A New Witness for Christ," *Ensign,* November 1984, 6–8.

5. Summaries of seventy of these maps are included in my *The Geography of Book of Mormon Events: A Source Book* (Provo, Utah: FARMS, 1992), 37–206.

6. See Orson Pratt, *Divine Authenticity of the Book of Mormon* (Liverpool: R. James, 1850), 22; Orson Pratt, in *Journal of Discourses,* 14:298. See also Orson Pratt's footnotes in the 1875 edition of the Book of Mormon, particularly 1 Nephi 18:23 n. k; Omni 1:12 n. g; and Omni 1:13 n. h.

7. See John Lloyd Stephens, *Incidents of Travel in Central America, Chiapas and Yucatan* (London: John Murray, 1841).

8. See "Extract from Stephens' 'Incidents of Travel in Central

America,'" *Times and Seasons* 3 (15 September 1842): 914–15, 921–22.

9. "To Subscribers," *Times and Seasons* 3 (15 March 1842): 710.

10. "Zarahemla," *Times and Seasons* 3 (1 October 1842): 927. Elder John A. Widtsoe observed, "The interesting fact . . . is that the Prophet Joseph Smith at this time was editor . . . and had announced his full editorial responsibility for the paper. This seems to give the . . . article an authority it might not otherwise possess." *Evidences and Reconciliations: Aids to Faith in a Modern Day* (Salt Lake City: Bookcraft, 1951), 3:96.

11. "Zarahemla," 927.

12. For example, Parley P. Pratt, *Key to the Science of Theology: A Voice of Warning* (Salt Lake City: Deseret Book, 1978), 15, said that "Lehi and Nephi came out with a colony from Jerusalem . . . and finally landed in safety on the coast of what is now called Chile, in South America." Pratt was absent from Nauvoo in the fall of 1842, and at that same time his brother Orson was also out of touch by virtue of his brief excommunication over the issue of polygamy.

13. George Q. Cannon, "Editorial Thoughts: The Book of Mormon Geography," *Juvenile Instructor* 25/1 (1 January 1890): 18.

14. George D. Pyper, "The Book of Mormon Geography," *The Instructor* 73 (April 1938): 160.

15. John A. Widtsoe, "Evidences and Reconciliations: Is Book of Mormon Geography Known?" *The Improvement Era* 53 (July 1950): 547.

16. John A. Widtsoe, foreword to *Cumorah—Where?* by Thomas Stuart Ferguson (Oakland: Author, 1947).

17. Joseph Fielding Smith, *Doctrines of Salvation*, comp. Bruce R. McConkie (Salt Lake City: Bookcraft, 1956), 3:203.

18. There is one often noted spot in the text that I believe is an editorial slip by Mormon (the 1979 edition eliminates the error). Alma 53:6 formerly read, "The city of Mulek which was one of the strongest holds of the Lamanites in the land of Nephi" (*Book of Mormon Critical Text: A Tool for Scholarly Reference*, [Provo, Utah:

FARMS, 1984], 2:849). Yet Alma 50:11 and 51:24–27 confirm that the city was actually part of the land of Zarahemla, which lay north of the land of Nephi. The textual mistake may have sprung from the fact that until shortly before this point in time, Lamanites had inhabited the Mulek area, called the "east wilderness." They were expelled by Moroni$_1$'s forces as a defensive measure (see Alma 50:7). Presumably, while Lamanites lived there, the city of Mulek and neighboring areas constituted de facto extensions of the Lamanite-ruled "land of Nephi" (Alma 22:28).

19.   See Sorenson, *Geography of Book of Mormon Events.*

20.   See, for example, *Webster's Third New International Dictionary of the English Language Unabridged,* s.v. "island," meaning 1a. The Hebrew term read in English as "isles of the sea" was used in the Bible to denote any lands that were "washed by the sea," including both the islands and coasts of the Mediterranean Sea (see LDS Bible Dictionary, 707), even when land access to those existed. Also see B. H. Roberts, "Remarks on the Foregoing Article," *The Improvement Era* 7 (February 1904): 267–79. Before Columbus's day, a Moorish noble referred to the Iberian peninsula as "this Island of Spain." L. P. Harvey, "Yuse Banegas: Un Moro noble en Granada bajo Los Reyes Católicos," *Al-Andalus* 21 (1956): 301.

21.   They also encountered Jaredite survivor Coriantumr near the east sea (see Omni 1:21; compare Ether 9:3; 15:11).

22.   The easterly position of the narrow pass is confirmed in references to the position of Teancum. It "lay in the borders by the seashore; and it was also near the city Desolation" (Mormon 4:3; see 4:2). In fact, it was adjacent to the city Desolation, which was at the narrow pass (see Mormon 3:5–6; 4:6–8, 13–14). Thus the city Desolation and the narrow pass were just one city away from the borders by the seashore, apparently only a short march distant. (While no statement is made that this was the east seashore, the geographical context points consistently toward that location but never toward the west seashore.)

23.   Someone might claim that Moroni$_1$ was designating by

these words all of North and South America, but the context provided by his situation and concern at the moment when he made the statement confirms the narrower meaning.

24. See Sorenson, *Geography of Book of Mormon Events,* 238–39.

25. Comparison of Alma 51:26 and 59:5 exposes what appears to be a scribal error. The former says that the Lamanites captured Nephihah in their first strike, but 59:5 has the place still in Nephite hands some five years later. I suppose that the historian listed Nephihah too hastily in the former passage, a natural enough response to the dismay felt at the smashing success of Amalickiah's initial campaign.

26. See Sorenson, *Geography of Book of Mormon Events,* 224–27.

27. When verse 25 says they reached "the land of Zarahemla," I suppose this refers to the local land near the city of Zarahemla rather than to the general land of Zarahemla, which began above the city of Manti. Had the latter meaning been intended, I think the record would have noted an additional few days for the final leg of their journey.

28. See John L. Sorenson, *An Ancient American Setting for the Book of Mormon* (Salt Lake City: Deseret Book and FARMS, 1985), 8–9; *Geography of Book of Mormon Events,* 393–97.

29. See Sorenson, *Ancient American Setting,* 193–97; *Geography of Book of Mormon Events,* 230.

30. The intricate question of the placement of the city of Aaron is discussed in Sorenson, *Geography of Book of Mormon Events,* 235.

31. See John E. Clark, "A Key for Evaluating Nephite Geographies: A Review of F. Richard Hauck, *Deciphering the Geography of the Book of Mormon,*" *FARMS Review of Books* 1 (1989): 35.

32. For example, George Reynolds, *A Complete Concordance of the Book of Mormon,* ed. Philip C. Reynolds (Salt Lake City: Deseret Book, 1976), 7, notes that "the name City of Aaron . . . appears from the context to apply to widely separate places."

33. For example, Clark, "Key for Evaluating Nephite Geographies," 30, suggests that "the failure to mention the east 'sea' is not

due to mere grammatical parallelism or elliptical thought based on word order," given that three rather parallel phrasings omit the word "sea": "east to the west sea" (Alma 22:32); "east even unto the west sea" (Alma 22:33); and "west sea, even unto the east" (Helaman 4:7). The phrase in Alma 22:32 thus seems to have omitted the word "sea" not by chance but by intention.

34. Many examples for individuals and groups are documented in my "The Problem of Establishing Distances," in *Geography of Book of Mormon Events*, 393–97.

35. See Louis-Jacques Dorais, "Some Notes on the Semantics of Eastern Eskimo Localizers," *Anthropological Linguistics* 13 (March 1971): 92.

36. See Eckhard Unger, "Ancient Babylonian Maps and Plans," *Antiquity* 9 (1935): 311–22.

37. Evon Z. Vogt, "Summary and Appraisal," in *Desarrollo Cultural de los Mayas*, ed. Evon Z. Vogt and Alberto Ruz L. (Mexico: Universidad Nacional Autónoma de México, 1971), 414.

38. For further examples and documentation of cultural variation in directional concepts and terminology, consult appendix C, "The Problem of Directions," in my *Geography of Book of Mormon Events*, 401–12.

39. For example, note the numbers of times the text uses various directional terms: east and west, 64; eastward and westward, 3; south and north, 65; southward and northward, 65.

40. See John L. Sorenson, "Seasonality of Warfare in the Book of Mormon and in Mesoamerica," in *Warfare in the Book of Mormon*, ed. Stephen D. Ricks and William J. Hamblin (Salt Lake City: Deseret Book and FARMS, 1990), 445–77.

41. See my article, "When Lehi's Party Arrived in the Land, Did They Find Others There?" *Journal of Book of Mormon Studies* 1/1 (1992): 1–4, 26–28.

42. See my article, "The Book of Mormon as a Mesoamerican Record," in *Book of Mormon Authorship Revisited: The Evidence for*

Ancient Origins, ed. Noel B. Reynolds (Provo, Utah: FARMS, 1997), 391–521.

43. David Wilkinson, "Central Civilization," in *Civilizations and World Systems: Studying World-Historical Change,* ed. Stephen K. Sanderson (Walnut Creek, Calif.: AltaMira Press, 1995), 47–48; see 46–74.

44. The best treatments of the concept of civilization are conveniently found in Sanderson, *Civilizations and World Systems.*

45. See Ze'ev Herzog, "Cities: Cities in the Levant," in *Anchor Bible Dictionary,* ed. David Noel Freedman (New York: Doubleday, 1992), 1:1031–43.

46. The Jerusalem of Lehi$_1$'s day has been hypothesized to have had a population on the order of twenty-five thousand. See Magen Broshi, "Estimating the Population of Ancient Jerusalem," *Biblical Archaeology Review* 4/2 (June 1978): 10–15.

47. See James F. Strange, "Nazareth," in *Anchor Bible Dictionary,* 4:1050–51.

48. See John L. Sorenson, "The Composition of Lehi's Family," in *By Study and also by Faith* (Salt Lake City: Deseret Book and FARMS, 1990), 2:174–96.

49. See E. B. Banning, "Towers," in *Anchor Bible Dictionary,* 6:622–24; Sorenson, *Ancient American Setting,* 171–74.

50. See A. Brent Merrill, "Nephite Captains and Armies," in *Warfare in the Book of Mormon,* 268–71.

51. See ibid., 165–66.

52. See Sorenson, "When Lehi's Party Arrived."

53. These points are discussed in greater detail in John L. Sorenson, "The 'Mulekites,'" *BYU Studies* 30/3 (1990): 6–22.

54. See John A. Tvedtnes, "Book of Mormon Tribal Affiliation and Military Castes," in *Warfare in the Book of Mormon,* 296–326.

Scripture Index

Mosiah

1:10, p. 32
2:1, p. 32
7–22, p. 56
7:4, p. 33
7:5–6, p. 72
7:22, pp. 88–89
8:7–8, p. 58
8:7–9, p. 55
8:8, pp. 21, 87, 90
8:12, p. 121
9:5–8, p. 74
9:6–7, p. 109
9:8, pp. 99, 109
9:9, p. 88
9:14, p. 88
10:8, p. 72
10:9, p. 87
11:9, pp. 99, 100
11:12, pp. 71, 99
11:13, p. 99
18:1–7, 31–34, p. 55
18:4, p. 56
18:4, 16, p. 74
18:31–34, p. 56
18:35, p. 96
19:6, p. 71
20:7–9, p. 72
20:7, 9, p. 34
21:17, pp. 111–12
21:25, p. 21
21:25–27, p. 55
21:26, p. 59
22:11, 13, pp. 35–36

22:16, pp. 72, 86
23:1–3, 25–26, p. 55
23:1–4, 19, p. 56
23:1–5, 25–35, p. 112
23:3–4, p. 86
23:19–20, p. 90
23:30, p. 86
23:30–31, 35, p. 72
23:30, 35, p. 90
23:31, p. 86
23:31–37, p. 87
24:1–2, pp. 34, 74
24:2, p. 74
24:7, p. 89
24:17–21, p. 3
24:18–25, p. 55
24:20–25, p. 56
24:25, p. 132 n. 27
28:12, p. 121

Alma

1:15, p. 94
2, p. 55
2:15, p. 35
2:15–20, p. 36
2:15–37, p. 61
2:17–20, p. 35
2:34, p. 12
2:35, p. 85
2:36, pp. 85–86
2:37, pp. 61–62, 87
3:2, pp. 61, 86, 88
3:20–23, p. 12
4:2, pp. 61, 88
4:2–3, p. 86

Subject Index

The Foundation for Ancient Research and Mormon Studies

The Foundation for Ancient Research and Mormon Studies (FARMS) encourages and supports research and publication about the Book of Mormon: Another Testament of Jesus Christ and other ancient scriptures.

FARMS is a nonprofit, tax-exempt educational foundation affiliated with Brigham Young University. Its main research interests in the scriptures include ancient history, language, literature, culture, geography, politics, religion, and law. Although research on such subjects is of secondary importance when compared with the spiritual and eternal messages of the scriptures, solid scholarly research can supply certain kinds of useful information, even if only tentatively, concerning many significant and interesting questions about the ancient backgrounds, origins, composition, and meanings of scripture.

The work of the Foundation rests on the premise that the Book of Mormon and other scriptures were written by prophets of God. Belief in this premise—in the divinity of scripture—is a matter of faith. Religious truths require divine witness to establish the faith of the believer. While scholarly research cannot replace that witness, such studies may reinforce and encourage individual testimonies by fostering understanding and appreciation of the scriptures. It is hoped that this information will help people to "come unto Christ" (Jacob 1:7) and to understand and take more seriously these ancient witnesses of the atonement of Jesus Christ, the Son of God.

The Foundation works to make interim and final reports about its research available widely, promptly, and economically, both in scholarly and in popular formats. FARMS publishes information about the Book of Mormon and other ancient scripture in the *Insights* newsletter, books and research papers, *FARMS Review of Books, Journal of Book of Mormon Studies,* reprints of published scholarly papers, and videos and audiotapes. FARMS also supports the preparation of the Collected Works of Hugh Nibley.

To facilitate the sharing of information, FARMS sponsors lectures, seminars, symposia, firesides, and radio and television broadcasts in which research findings are communicated to working scholars and to anyone interested in faithful, reliable information about the scriptures. Through Research Press, a publishing arm of the Foundation, FARMS publishes materials addressed primarily to working scholars.

For more information about the Foundation and its activities, contact the FARMS office at 1-800-327-6715 or (801) 373-5111. You can also visit the FARMS Web site at http://farms.byu.edu.

FARMS PUBLICATIONS

Teachings of the Book of Mormon

The Geography of Book of Mormon Events: A Source Book

The Book of Mormon Text Reformatted according to Parallelistic
   Patterns

Eldin Ricks's Thorough Concordance of the LDS Standard Works

A Guide to Publications on the Book of Mormon: A Selected
   Annotated Bibliography

Book of Mormon Authorship Revisited: The Evidence for Ancient
   Origins

Ancient Scrolls from the Dead Sea: Photographs and Commentary on a
   Unique Collection of Scrolls

LDS Perspectives on the Dead Sea Scrolls

Isaiah in the Book of Mormon

King Benjamin's Speech: "That Ye May Learn Wisdom"

Mormons, Scripture, and the Ancient World: Studies in Honor of
   John L. Sorenson

Latter-day Christianity: Ten Basic Issues

Illuminating the Sermon at the Temple and Sermon on the Mount

Scripture Study: Tools and Suggestions

Finding Biblical Hebrew and Other Ancient Literary Forms in the Book
   of Mormon

Charting the Book of Mormon: Visual Aids for Personal Study and
   Teaching

Pressing Forward with the Book of Mormon: The FARMS Updates of
   the 1990s

King Benjamin's Speech Made Simple

Romans 1: Notes and Reflections

The Temple in Time and Eternity

Periodicals

Insights: A Window on the Ancient World

FARMS Review of Books

Journal of Book of Mormon Studies

Reprint Series

Book of Mormon Authorship: New Light on Ancient Origins

The Doctrine and Covenants by Themes

Offenders for a Word

Copublished with Deseret Book Company

An Ancient American Setting for the Book of Mormon
Warfare in the Book of Mormon
By Study and Also by Faith: Essays in Honor of Hugh W. Nibley
The Sermon at the Temple and the Sermon on the Mount
Rediscovering the Book of Mormon
Reexploring the Book of Mormon
Of All Things! Classic Quotations from Hugh Nibley
The Allegory of the Olive Tree
Temples of the Ancient World
Expressions of Faith: Testimonies from LDS Scholars
Feasting on the Word: The Literary Testimony of the Book of Mormon

The Collected Works of Hugh Nibley
Old Testament and Related Studies
Enoch the Prophet
The World and the Prophets
Mormonism and Early Christianity
Lehi in the Desert; The World of the Jaredites; There Were Jaredites
An Approach to the Book of Mormon
Since Cumorah
The Prophetic Book of Mormon
Approaching Zion
The Ancient State
Tinkling Cymbals and Sounding Brass
Temple and Cosmos
Brother Brigham Challenges the Saints

Published through Research Press

Pre-Columbian Contact with the Americas across the Oceans:
    An Annotated Bibliography
A Comprehensive Annotated Book of Mormon Bibliography
New World Figurine Project, vol. 1
Images of Ancient America: Visualizing Book of Mormon Life
Chiasmus in Antiquity (reprint)
Chiasmus Bibliography

Publications of the FARMS Center for the Preservation of Ancient Religious Texts

The Incoherence of the Philosophers
Dead Sea Scrolls Electronic Reference Library